9780956281500

D1743618

# The Leicestershire Coleopterists

## by
## Derek Lott

**Loughborough Naturalists' Club**

*To Beverley,*
*Anne and Asress,*
*John and Jacqui*

Published by the Loughborough Naturalists' Club

© 2009 Derek Lott

ISBN 978-0-9562815-0-0

Printed by the Lighthouse Colour Division of Barrow Reprographics

# Contents

# Acknowledgments

I am indebted to Beverley Heath of Leicestershire and Rutland Wildlife Trust for designing this book and to Katherin Ward, who sorted out copyright issues and sourced the majority of the illustrations and photographs. I am grateful to the Loughborough Naturalists' Club for funding its publication and in particular to Helen Ikin, who acted as its champion. Financial help was also received from the Leicestershire Entomological Society. I am also grateful to Ian Evans, who originally collected a significant amount of the information, on which this book is based and who persuaded me to write things down. Peter Gamble, Jan Dawson, Mary Hider, Roger Clark, Michael Darby, A.A. Allen and R.R.U. Kaufmann also provided leads and snippets of information. Anona Finch, Tony Fletcher and Darwyn Sumner at Leicestershire County Council kindly provided access to the collections, library and numerous files after I left gainful employment there. I am similarly grateful to staff at the Natural History Museum, the Royal Entomological Society, Charles MacKechnie-Jarvis and Garth Foster for access to manuscript material. Jon Daws, Jeremy Woodhead, Tony Drane, Pete Kirby, Mark Mawson and many other naturalists contributed large numbers of modern beetle specimens and records, which, along with electronic collection catalogues made by Trevor Forsythe, were used to assess the faunal changes described in this book. I received encouragement to continue and write up my studies from numerous people including Tony Drane, Ray Morris and Roger Key. Thanks to John Ward, who proof-read the entire manuscript and to Anne Asfaw, who constructed the index.

## Illustrations

**Front cover**
Drawing of beetle made by Claude Henderson (by permission of Katherin Ward)
**Title page**
Claude Henderson (by permission of the Loughborough Naturalists' Club)
**Back cover**
The author searching for water beetles at Puddledyke near Cropston (by permission of Leicestershire and Rutland Wildlife Trust)
**Plates**
i.   Map of Leicestershire and Rutland (designed by Anne Asfaw, drawn by Geof Yarwood)
    A scene in Bradgate Park (by permission of Collections Resources Centre, Leicestershire County Council Environment and Heritage Services)
ii.  Frontispiece from Bates' *The Naturalist on the River Amazons* (by permission of the trustees of the National Library of Scotland)
iii. H. Donisthorpe at the BM (by permission of Natural History Museum, London); Henry Walter Bates (by permission of Record Office for Leicester, Leicestershire and Rutland); S.O. Taylor (by permission of Collections Resources Centre, Leicestershire County Council Environment and Heritage Servicess); Frank Bouskell (by permission of Record Office for Leicester, Leicestershire and Rutland)
iv.  Claude Henderson and Don Tozer (by permission of Jan Dawson)
v.   Drawings of beetles made by Claude Henderson (by permission of Katherin Ward)
vi.  A drawer from the Henderson Collection (by permission of Collections Resources Centre, Leicestershire County Council Environment and Heritage Services)
    Musk Beetle (by permission of Roger Key)
vii. Ancient oak at Bradgate Park (by permission of Leicestershire and Rutland Wildlife Trust)
viii. The ground beetle, *Calosoma inquisitor* (by permission of Frank Köhler)
    Green Tiger Beetle (by permission of Roger Key)
The publishers have made every effort to trace copyright ownership and would be grateful to learn of any unwitting copyright infringement.

# *Introduction*

On Christmas Eve 1991 I was walking into Leicester Market to buy provisions for the Christmas dinner, when I came across a commotion on the corner of the market place. A small crowd was standing around an old man who had fallen off his push-bike and was unable to get up owing to infirmity and a long-standing lameness. I recognised him immediately as Don Tozer, one of the old Leicestershire beetle collectors, and asked him what he was doing lying on his back in the middle of the street. Being a highly independent character, Don was chiefly concerned that people should go away and "*not make a fuss*". Assuming that I was in some way responsible for him, the crowd expressed disapproval of my negligence and eventually dissipated. Having assured me that he was quite capable of cycling home with his vegetables, if I could help him onto his bike, Don cycled off into the distance, not quite in a straight line.

Don was one of the kindest men I have ever met. He had an immense knowledge of local beetles and was always willing to impart that knowledge to people like me who were just starting their studies. In doing so, Don was following a long-established tradition of camaraderie among beetle collectors. He was a link in a chain that stretched all the way back to the great Victorian naturalist, Henry Walter Bates, who studied Leicestershire beetles in the 1840s. Don was introduced to the study of beetles in the 1920s by Oliver Taylor, who in turn was helped in the 1900s by Frank Bouskell, who in the 1890s collected in Charnwood Forest with Frederick Bates, who was the younger brother of Henry Bates.

This book tells the story of a remarkable set of people, the Leicestershire coleopterists. They looked more closely at their natural surroundings than most and were rewarded by finding a hidden world populated by thousands of species of bizarre creatures. They came from all walks of life, but they were united by their sense of enquiry and fascination. Their passion for beetles led some of them on voyages of discovery to such exotic places as Brazil, Madagascar and the wintry wastes of islands in the South Atlantic. Records of their work in the form of collections, manuscripts and scientific notes and papers inform us of changes in Leicestershire's biodiversity over 200 years. Their studies tell us that some species have become rare or died out and that others have moved in. Together with other naturalists who pursued their interests in other groups of plants and animals, they built up a body of knowledge that provides a basis for the modern conservation movement.

The study of Leicestershire beetles has proceeded in bursts of activity carried out by successive generations of coleopterists. Consequently, the narrative of this book is divided into periods of time that coincide with these episodes: 1782-1793, 1840-1860, 1861-1892, 1893-1907. 1908-1959 and 1960-1981. Postscripts cover recorded changes in the county beetle fauna over 200 years and notes on the main Leicestershire beetle collections. The term, Leicestershire, as used here, refers to the botanical recording unit of vice-county and so includes Rutland.

# 1782 – 1795  Crabbe

The agricultural revolution in the eighteenth century gave rise to a new interest in insects as pests. In a treatise on farming in the Midland counties, Marshall (1790) included several descriptions of insects causing damage to crops. It could be argued that his observation of *chafers* defoliating a wood near Breedon on 13th June 1784 constitutes the earliest known record of a beetle in Leicestershire and Rutland. Although it is likely that this observation refers to the cockchafer, *Melolontha melolontha*, sufficient uncertainty attaches to the identity of the species of chafer for us to look to a true naturalist, the Reverend George Crabbe, for the oldest known observations of beetles in Leicestershire.

Crabbe (1754-1832) is better known as the poet from Aldeburgh, Suffolk, who wrote *Peter Grimes*, but he was also an ardent naturalist and was domestic chaplain to the Duke of Rutland in the Vale of Belvoir for some years (Darby 2006). According to Lisney (1960), he was at Belvoir Castle between 1782 and 1785, then Stathern until 1789 and Muston until 1793. His *Natural History of the Vale of Belvoir* (Crabbe 1790) is an extraordinary achievement for its time and covers geology, botany and zoology. The section on beetles is particularly strong. It uses scientific binomial names and refers to major contemporary works by Linnaeus and Fabricius. A useful commentary on this work is provided by Donisthorpe (1896), who gives opinions on the identities of the species names used by Crabbe. 41 beetle species are listed from the Vale of Belvoir and many of these can be confidently related to modern species names, including the Lesser Stag Beetle, *Dorcus parallelipipedus*, the Musk Beetle, *Aromia moschata* and the Violet Ground Beetle, *Carabus violaceus*. Several species, such as the Green Tiger Beetle, *Cicindela campestris*, the oil beetle, *Meloe proscarabaeus*, and the ground beetle, *Calosoma inquisitor* are no longer known from the Vale. These species may have been relicts of a pre-inclosure landscape that in the first half of the eighteenth century included large tracts of forest for hunting (Honeybone 1987). Crabbe's assertion that the Stag Beetle, *Lucanus cervus*, did not occur there is of particular value, given the number of spurious Leicestershire records generated in succeeding centuries.

*The Natural History of the Vale of Belvoir* was first published by Nichols in 1790 without accreditation to Crabbe. It was later reprinted by Nichols *verbatim*, except for accreditation to the author (Crabbe 1795) and it is in this latter format that it is more widely known following its reissue in a facsimile edition in 1976.

Crabbe built up an important beetle collection, long since lost, which was referred to by Marsham (1802) and Stephens (1828). He returned to Muston between 1805 and 1814, but if his interest in entomology continued, no record of his findings has survived. In fact no other observations of beetles in Leicestershire and Rutland are known until 1840.

# *1840 – 1860 Bates and friends*

The 1840s witnessed a flowering of entomological activity that had its roots in the coincidence of three historical events. Firstly, the Leicester Literary and Philosophical Society (LLPS) was founded in 1835 and, together with other educational bodies such as the Mechanics Institute, provided opportunities for a whole new social class to take up academic studies and receive practical support and encouragement for their activities. Secondly, the publication of a guide to British beetles by Stephens (1839) made it easier for naturalists to identify beetles down to specific level with the aid of a hand lens. The last and perhaps the most important event was the appearance on the scene in 1842 of a dynamic seventeen-year-old called Henry Walter Bates, whose energy and enthusiasm was infectious and inspirational to a new generation of entomologists.

At the age of 13, Bates became apprenticed to a hosier and by the age of 15 he was working an eleven hour day before studying Greek and Latin at evening classes (Moon 1976). It appears that he also had time to walk out to Charnwood Forest, collect beetles, identify them and write up the results, because in 1843 he published the first note on Leicestershire beetles since Crabbe. His *Note on coleopterous insects frequenting damp places* (Bates, H.W. 1843) appeared in Volume One of the Zoologist, a new journal that later hosted a number of notes on Leicestershire beetles by Bates and his contemporaries. In his writings, Bates displayed an industrious enthusiasm for entomology. According to his brother (Bates, F. 1892):

*"Never shall I forget his radiant joy ... when he once came bounding in, shouting in exultation, with his first capture of a 'Tiger' beetle, made in Anstey Lane... Our earliest collections, I well remember, were stored away in such places as table and wash-hand stand drawers. Our collecting nets too were very primitive - a loop of wire soldered into a tin socket to hold a stick... My brother used habitually to write a descriptive account of all these expeditions; he would also sketch and write out descriptions of all the principal insects captured".*

A fascinating insight into the naturalist's world at this time is given by the diaries of James Harley kept between 1840 and 1844. Harley was a very competent and active naturalist. He produced a list of birds recorded in Leicestershire (Harley 1840) and his observation on July 22nd 1840 of a glow worm at Newtown Linford is the earliest nineteenth century Leicestershire beetle record known to me. In his diaries we read a narrative of long excursions into the countryside, conducted on foot. It was not unusual for Harley to rise at 5am in order to spend the whole day in Charnwood Forest, his favourite hunting grounds away from the environs of Leicester. The nearest Forest locality to Leicester is Bradgate Park and many of his observations were made there or along Anstey Lane, the road leading to it. Harley corresponded frequently and at length with fellow naturalists around Britain. Evidently, the mail was very efficient and his correspondents were very prompt, because he often received a reply two days after writing.

Local naturalists had obviously collected insects before the 1840s. In 1841 the museum of the LLPS purchased *"several cases of stuffed birds and insects from the collections of the late Mrs Abney"* (Museum report 1841). Mrs Abney possibly represents one of the last examples of an eighteenth century vogue for ladies of society to keep collections (Thomas 1983). She seems to have been highly regarded and Harley writes on July 25th 1840:

*"Mrs Abney gives me a kind invitation to her house to inspect her treasures in art, natural history and paintings".*

Collecting was probably also carried out by less advantaged social classes. Holyoak (1906) described James Bond, a hosiery worker, as *"the father of entomology"* at this time and stated that he taught Bates the art of taking and preserving bird skins.

On June 17th 1841, Harley sent the first of several boxes of Leicestershire beetles off to one of his correspondents, Professor MacGillivray of Aberdeen, for identification. This and frequent observations of butterflies, dragonflies and beetles attest to his interest in entomology. However, he was persistently imprecise in his use of Linnaean nomenclature for the insects that he recorded in his diaries. Many beetles were referred to by a rather broad generic name, e.g. *Elater*, while species of *Geotrupes* are sometimes represented simply by their specific name, e.g. *vernalis*. Using Stephens' manual, Bates was able to adopt a consistent binomial nomenclature and identify beetles down to species and in this way he and his followers have given us the earliest sensible picture of Leicestershire's beetle fauna.

The earliest known reference to Bates as a naturalist is as a sixteen-year-old in Harley's diary entry for April 6th 1841:

*"Young Bates informed me that ardea cinerea* [the heron] *used a few years since to nestle in Bilsdon Coplow Wood".*

On June 19th:

*"Bates captures Libellula maculata in Anstey Lane. Knapp in his Journal of a Naturalist speaks of this dragonfly as being very rare".*

On June 21st:

*"Mr Bates read a paper to the members of the Natural History class on the structure and functions of insects. Very interesting".*

It appears from the diary that Bates may have been Harley's pupil on a course of classes, perhaps run at the Mechanic's Institute. Clearly, Bates was making his mark and it would be no surprise if such a precocious talent in someone so young and of somewhat inferior social class caused some insecurity in his teacher. On July 3rd 1841, Harley alludes to Bates with mild sarcasm as *"Prof. Bates"*. On September 2nd:

*"Conversation with Mr Rylands* [regarding] *the difference of opinion of the Natural History Class. Bates declared in error. Considered a mere boy".*

On April 26th 1842, Harley, who was prone to occasional vents of spleen, was moved to write:

*"Drew a line of demarcation between Kirby, Bates and the class! Kirby an ignorant fellow! Bates better but low bred and dreggy. Ignobleness and ignorance ought to be left behind in the swamp of low life when they wish to be identified with the intelligent of our kind. There are however metals so gross that no fusion or retort or alembic will refine!!"*

This is the last mention of Bates by Harley and perhaps represents a rupture in relations that lasted until the diary was discontinued at the end of 1844.

By this time, Bates was well advanced in his exploration of the Leicestershire beetle fauna. In a report of the Museum Committee of the LLPS dated October 3rd 1842, it was reported:

*"Of about 4,000 species of Coleoptera described as British, at least 2,000 have been discovered in Leicestershire during researches continued but for a few months".*

These figures may be somewhat exaggerated, but they do reflect the extraordinarily fast progress made by Bates in his studies. His eloquent writings display an enterprising approach to collecting and include what may be one of the first published references (Bates, H.W. 1844) to the collection of beetles from flood refuse:

*"We are well situated in time of floods, for our numerous watercourses, from the narrowness or elevation of their beds, readily overflow and the contents of many a broad acre are swept along with the turbid waters :- Rapidus vorat aequore vortex. Apparent rari (multi) nantes in gurgite vasto. The town serves us for a riddle, through which the waters are sifted, and the living sediment is deposited on the hedges and fences which oppose its progress. Here we have taken about a fourth of the British Harpalidae".*

Altogether Henry Bates contributed nine papers on Leicestershire beetles (containing 123 individual records) to the pages of the Zoologist between 1843 and 1848, while his comrade-in-arms from the Mechanics Institute, Kirby, published a single note in 1845 containing records of 33 beetle species mainly from Sheet Hedges Wood and its neighbourhood. A few more Kirby records turn up in later manuscript lists.

It is unclear how closely Bates collaborated with John Plant, another contributor to our knowledge of Leicestershire beetles in the 1840s. Plant was five years older than Henry Bates and was mentioned almost from the start of Harley's diaries in 1840. He features frequently, but always separately from Bates, and appears to have developed a wide range of interests. Between 1845 and 1850, he compiled a catalogue of Leicestershire Mollusca (Mott 1887). He published several notes on a variety of subjects in the Zoologist, including a *Note on the comparative numbers of Coleoptera affecting meadow lands* (Plant, J. 1844b), which listed the numbers of specimens in each family collected from refuse left by the same floods that had provided Bates with such rich pickings. He highlighted several rare species including *Hydrochus brevis*. From the nomenclature used in his species list, it appears that Plant used Stephens' earlier works as much as the *Manual* used by Bates. There is little evidence of any further activity on beetles by John Plant. He gave a beetle to Frederick Bates in 1848 and he may have been the "I. Plant" who collected an exotic species of *Serropalpus* from Charnwood Forest (Westwood 1844). In February 1843, he was appointed the first curator of the LLPS museum (Lott 1935), soon after a museum entomology department was set up in October 1842, but he left within two years.

A minute of a LLPS meeting of January 28th 1845 *"proposed that a curator be appointed in the room of Mr Plant who has resigned."* After working at the Permanent Library, he left Leicester in 1849 to become curator of Salford Museum, where he concentrated on Geology and Palaeontology and became a Major in the Salford Corps of Volunteers (Anon 1892).

Henry Bates undoubtedly inspired many others to take up the study of Leicestershire beetles. In Leicester Library in1844 he met the young Alfred Wallace, who was then teaching in Leicester for two years, and persuaded him to take up entomology (Wallace 1905). One of his protégés was his younger brother, Frederick Bates, who later described excursions to Charnwood Forest, with a season beginning on Good Friday (Bales, F. 1892). Sometimes these outings became social occasions referred to by participants as gypsy parties (Holyoak 1906). The younger Bates' collection register for 1848 to 1849 survives (though not, alas, his collection) and contains some interesting notes on collecting activities at that time. Several areas of Bradgate Park and Anstey Lane are described and given names such as "*Elater* Spinney" and "*Poecilus* Field", presumably following prized captures. From these notes and from the localities given in his register, it is apparent that Bradgate Park was a highly favoured collecting ground for local entomologists. Frederick Bates also received Leicestershire specimens from a large number of people named in the register and several of these obviously kept their own collections. Aside from Kirby and John Plant, none of these collectors left any collections or publications that have survived to our time, but some names turn up in other contemporary records. A donation of *"upwards of 300 coleopterous insects taken in Leicestershire"* on November 5th 1849 by E. Glover is recorded in the Leicester Museum Accessions Ledger and Glover acted as museum curator between July and September 1851.

The museum had by then been taken over by Leicester Corporation, but the rapid turn-over of curators seems to have continued, no doubt partly in consequence of the close interest in the details of the curator's work by enthusiastic members of the committee with high expectations. The accessions ledger also records a donation of beetles including a coastal species, *Phaleria cadaverina*, by J.D. Moore on July 25th 1856. D. Moore gave some Leicestershire beetles to Frederick Bates in 1849, but also many more from Hastings and it is possible that he was a Sussex coleopterist who visited Leicestershire. On 8th October 1849 the museum received 1,051 British insects from Thomas Marshall Esq. including 445 Coleoptera. Marshall was regarded as something of an authority on insects at the time. He was an honorary curator at the museum and named some beetles for Frederick Bates in 1848. We know nothing of any work that he did on Leicestershire beetles himself, but some of his local records of bugs (Hemiptera) appeared in later works (Clements & Evans 1973).

In 1848, Henry Bates set sail for Brazil with Alfred Wallace. After pioneering work collecting specimens on the Amazon, both of them went on to achieve celebrated places in the history of science. Bates described the phenomenon whereby harmless species mimic harmful species and gain protection from predators (now called Batesian mimicry), while Wallace's essays on variation finally persuaded Darwin to publish his own theory of natural selection in order to avoid being beaten to it.

When Henry Bates eventually returned to England, he worked in London and took no further active part in Leicestershire entomology, although he did remain an entomological icon in his native county. Frederick, however, stayed in Leicester in the brewery business and played a major role in the local scene at various times. Between 1849 and 1854 he published five notes in the Zoologist containing 81 of his Leicestershire records. In these notes, he employed a similar florid prose to that of his elder brother. For example, when describing the collection of the carrion beetle, *Necrodes littoralis*, from the remains of a dead horse (Bates, F. 1852):

*"It was an exhilarating sight to see me, with beaming countenance, bending over these remains, puffing out huge volumes of smoke from my meerschaum [pipe], in order to keep the effluvium (not small I assure you) off my stomach; ever and anon diving with my fingers into the unctious mass, to secure the Necrodes which were rolling and rollicking about, evidently luxuriating in their filthy feast."*

Bates exchanged specimens with many other British coleopterists and for the next few years, several taxonomic revisions refer to specimens collected by F. Bates in Leicestershire.

The 1850s also witnessed the emergence of another Leicestershire coleopterist, the enigmatic Francis Plant, who was the younger brother of John Plant. Frank Plant, as he was known, was a bookbinder, who kept an insect breeding cage on his bench so that he could *"note the many changes that went on among his pets"* (Holyoak 1906). He is first mentioned in 1854 as a collecting companion of Frederick Bates, but it is not known when he started collecting, nor when he was born. He was probably one of the *"brothers Plant"* mentioned as present at Henry Bates' farewell party at Bradgate Park in 1848 (Holyoak 1906) and it is tempting to speculate that he could have been the *"young entomologist"* who provided Kirby with records of *Donacia* (reed beetles) from Misterton in 1845 (Kirby 1845), although there is no direct evidence for this. He was obviously a highly gifted collector and succeeded in adding *Tropideres sepicola* to the British list (Janson 1857). Only 30 of his records have been passed down to us, but it is clear that he had a knack of finding cryptic species such as the aquatic leaf beetle, *Macroplea appendiculata*, from Groby Pool (Plant, F. 1857), never since recorded in Leicestershire, and the weevil, *Trachodes hispidus* (Bates, F. 1854), obtained by beating sticks lying on the ground. He also tended to be more wide-ranging in his collecting localities. Other collectors of the period concentrated almost exclusively on Charnwood Forest and the immediate environs of Leicester, where they lived. According to Henry Bates (1844b):

*"The best places for collecting are the old damp woods, sandy and heathy lanes and waste grounds on the forest or N.W. side of the county. An entomologist would be guilty of a great mistake, if he should think of finding anything on the cold, woodless pasture lands that accompany the lias formation of the eastern side of Leicestershire".*

Frank Plant gained permission to visit land owned by the Midland Railway Company (Plant, F. 1857) and explored new areas, previously unvisited by other entomologists. Perhaps his greatest contribution to knowledge was the discovery of Buddon Wood as a site of outstanding entomological interest. His captures there of *Tropideres sepicola* and *Trachodes hispidus* helped to establish the site as one of the premier collecting localities in the Midlands.

The main protagonists mentioned so far were all based in the town of Leicester and there is very little evidence of activities emanating from anywhere else in the county. On December 22nd 1840, Harley records walking from Leicester over Charnwood Forest to Loughborough in order to give a paper on the British hirundines to members of the Loughborough Natural History Society, but there is no mention of any entomological activity within that town. William Turner of Uppingham in Rutland published several entomological notes in the Zoologist, but none concerned beetles [1]. The nearest major centre of entomological activity to Leicester at this time was Burton on Trent in Staffordshire, which remained a breeding ground for coleopterists throughout the century. At this time, Edwin Brown was the coleopterist in residence. Harley corresponded with him and on September 7th 1842 visited Burton on Trent with John Plant for a meeting, when they availed themselves of the new railway, recently opened. Harley described a museum at Burton as being "*well arranged*". Henry Bates actually worked in Burton for a year through a connection with Brown (Moon 1976) and published a note on the beetles he captured there.

In addition to the home-grown coleopterists mentioned above, other visiting entomologists also collected beetles in Leicestershire at this time, including two national figures. The eminent coleopterist, John Power, was actually born in Leicestershire at Market Bosworth, but lived most of his life in London (Dunning 1886). Power's father and grandfather were both interested in Botany and he himself collected plants in Leicestershire from the age of 14 up until 1837 (Horwood & Noel 1933). He is better known, however, as a celebrated and influential beetle collector who, contrary to contemporary practice, kept long series of each species from several localities (MacKechnie Jarvis 1976). Consequently, he built up what is probably the most important collection of British beetles in the mid nineteenth century, now to be found in the British collection in the Natural History Museum (London). He made two beetle collecting trips to Charnwood Forest in August 1855 and July 1860. Fifty-three beetle records can be gleaned from the entries in his register as well as some records of Heteroptera (plant bugs). T. V. Wollaston was another notable collector who came to Leicestershire. He was a consumptive and visited Madeira several times for a cure, where he carried out pioneering work on the unique insect fauna of the island (Salmon & Wakeham-Dawson 1999). He had family connections with Shenton Hall, also near Market Bosworth, from where he made occasional collecting forays to Ambion Wood. Sixteen of his Leicestershire captures are cited mainly in various taxonomic reviews of the period. He discovered two species new to Britain from Shenton Hall itself: *Atomaria peltata* and *Clitostethus arcuatus*. Lastly, four "*Leicester*" records appear in annotations to a copy of Stephens' manual made by Thomas Pigg and kindly transcribed for me by Tony Drane. The records are attributed to J.P. Bartlett, who, judging from other annotations, may have been a Northampton-based collector.

[1] It is interesting to note that one of these was on the capture of a locust. No less than eight specimens of locally captured locusts were presented to Leicester Museum between 1849 and 1860.

The flurry of coleopterological activity that started with Henry Bates resulted in the preparation of the first catalogue of Leicestershire Coleoptera in 1854 by his brother, Frederick (Donisthorpe 1903). Originally this was written for a History of Leicestershire to be edited by T.R. Potter (Mott 1887). Unfortunately, this was never published (Bates, F. 1879), and although the catalogue was placed for reference in the library of Leicester Museum, it is now lost. Through the kindness of Mr Charles MacKechnie Jarvis, I have been able to view a copy of Sharp's published catalogue of British Coleoptera, which has been annotated by Bates with Leicestershire records. Clearly this includes at least some of the records used to compile the 1854 catalogue, but it is not possible to distinguish most of them with confidence from records made at a later date. In these annotations, Bates records that the list was dated April 19th 1854 and listed 790 species in 286 genera.

This productive period in Leicestershire came to an end around 1860 when many of the collectors of the previous two decades appear to have stopped collecting in Leicestershire. Frank Plant sailed to Madagascar, no doubt inspired by Henry Bates and his brother, Nathaniel Plant, who had followed Bates to Brazil in the 1850s. From Madagascar, Plant wrote a letter to the dealer, Samuel Stevens, published in the Zoologist (Plant, F. 1863). Sadly, within five years, he had died of smallpox (Anon 1892) and the skills of a highly talented collector were extinguished and passed into obscurity largely unrecorded. Frederick Bates (1879) reported that:

*"The neat and handsome little collection of Mr Plant was offered at a cheap rate to our Museum, but was not taken; the committee I suppose not being able to discern any value in 'beetles', even though they were a part of our local fauna, the obtaining of which ought to be one of the prime considerations in the formation and management of a local museum".*

Bates himself turned his attention to worldwide beetles, orchids and freshwater algae and largely abandoned Leicestershire Coleoptera for 35 years, citing problems of access to Bradgate Park following the death of its owner, the Old Earl of Stamford (Bates, F. 1879).

# Coleopterists active in Leicestershire 1840 to 1860

| Name | Born | Died | Active in Leics | Main biographic sources |
|---|---|---|---|---|
| J.P. Bartlett | ? | ? | 1848 | Pigg annotations |
| Frederick Bates | 28.11.1829 | 6.10.1903 | 1848-1896 | Bates (1879), Donisthorpe (1903) |
| Henry Walter Bates | 8.2.1825 | 16.2.1892 | 1842-1848 | Moon (1976), Harley MS, Holyoak (1906) |
| B. Bond | ? | ? | 1849 | Bates register |
| W. Bond | ? | ? | 1849 | Bates register |
| C. Boswell | ? | ? | 1848-1849 | Bates register |
| E. Glover | ? | ? | 1849 | Museum Accessions Register, Bates register |
| T.B. Kirby (initials also given as H.B.) | ? | ? | 1845-1848 | Harley MS, Bates register |
| J.D. Moore | ? | ? | 1849 | Bates register |
| Francis Plant | ? | c1865 | 1854-1860 | Plant (1863), Anon (1892), Holyoak (1906) |
| John Plant | 10.1819 | 1.1894 | 1844-1848 | Anon (1892), Hudleston (1894), Harley MS |
| John Arthur Power | 18.3.1810 | 10.6.1886 | 1855, 1860 | Dunning (1886), MacKechnie Jarvis (1976) |
| Alfred Russell Wallace | 8.1.1823 | 6.11.1913 | 1845-1848 | Moon (1976) |
| Thomas Vernon Wollaston | 1822 | 1878 | c1854-1872 | |

# Manuscript sources for the period 1840-1860

Leicester Museum Accessions Ledger (Leicester City Museums Service)
Frederick Bates' Old Register (Natural History Museum, London)
Frederick Bates' annotations of Sharp's catalogue (C. MacKechnie Jarvis)
Register of Power Collection (Natural History Museum, London)
James Harley's Diary of a Naturalist 1840-1844 (Leics Record Office)
LLPS Museum Reports (Leics Record Office - 14D55/59/1-2)
LLPS General minutes 1844-1885 (Leics Record Office - 14D55/1)
Thomas Pigg's annotations of Stephens' manual (A.B. Drane)

# Main literature sources for Leicestershire beetle records 1840-1860

ANON. (1856). Exhibitions. Proceedings of the entomological Society of London August 4th 1856.

BATES, F. (1849). Capture of coleopterous insects in light sandy situations. *Zoologist* **7**: 2437-2439.

BATES, F. (1852). Method of obtaining *Trox sabulosus. Zoologist* **10**: 3375-3376.

BATES, F. (1852). Occurrence of *Necrodes littoralis* in considerable numbers. *Zoologist* **10**: 3376.

BATES, F. (1852). Occurrence of *Carabus arvensis* in Leicestershire. *Zoologist* **10**: 3376.

BATES, F. (1854). Captures in Leicestershire. *Zoologist* **12**: 4437-4438.

BATES, H.W. (1843). Notes on coleopterous insects frequenting damp places. *Zoologist* **1**: 114-115.

BATES, H.W. (1844). Notes on the habits of Coleoptera. *Zoologist* **2**: 410-412.

BATES, H.W. (1844). Note on *Epaphius secalis. Zoologist* **2**: 476.

BATES, H.W. (1844). Notes on *Ocys melanocephalus. Zoologist* **2**: 476.

BATES, H.W. (1844). Notes on the habits of *Hylesinus fraxini* (Fab.). *Zoologist* **2**: 610-611.

BATES, H.W. (1844). Note on the captures of rarer Coleoptera in Leicestershire. *Zoologist* **2**: 410-412.

BATES, H.W. (1845). Notes on *Epaphius secalis* etc. *Zoologist* **3**: 1094-1095.

BATES, H.W. (1846). Distribution of the species of *Harpalus* and *Ophonus. Zoologist* **4**: 1236.

BATES, H.W. (1848). Remarks on local species of Coleoptera in the neighbourhood of Burton on Trent. *Zoologist* **6**: 1997-1999.

BROWN, E. (1863). The fauna and flora of the district surrounding Tutbury and Burton on Trent. In: O. Mosley. *The Natural History of Tutbury.*

CLARK, H. (1856). Synopsis: list of the British species of *Philhydra* with notices of localities etc. *Zoologist* **14**: 5048-5056.

CLARK, H. (1862). Description of species of the genus *Hydroporus* Clair, new to the European or British catalogues. Journal of Entomology **1**: 468-474.

DAWSON, J.F. (1856). Notes on British Geodephaga with description of one new species (supplementary to *Geodephaga Britannica*). *Entomologist's Annual* **1856**: 65-81.

DAWSON, J.F. (1857). Notes on British Geodephaga with description of four new species (supplementary to *Geodephaga Britannica*). *Entomologist's Annual* **1857**: 61-68.

HARRIS, J.S. (1860). Capture of *Trachodes hispidus* in Leicestershire. *Zoologist* **18**: 7218.

KIRBY, H.B. (1845). Capture of coleopterous insects in Leicestershire. *Zoologist* **3**: 1094.

PLANT, F. (1857). Captures of Coleoptera in Leicestershire. *Zoologist* **15**: 5544-5545.

PLANT, F. (1860). Capture of *Tropideres sepicola. Zoologist* **18**: 7218.

PLANT, J. (1844). Note on the comparative numbers of Coleoptera affecting meadow lands. *Zoologist* **2**: 475-476.

POWER, J.A. (1856). Notes on the genus *Haliplus. Zoologist* **14**: 5174-5178.

RYE, E.C. (1866). Occurrence of *Hylurgops pilosus. Entomologist's monthly Magazine* **2**: 258-259.

WATERHOUSE, G.R. (1862). Descriptions of British species of the genus *Gyrophaena. Transactions of the entomological Society of London* (3rd Series) **1**: 241-252.

WATERHOUSE, G.R. & JANSON, E.W. (1855). British species of the genus *Stenus. Transactions of the entomological Society of London* (New Series) **3**: 136-156.

WESTWOOD, J.O. (1844). Notice of the occurrence of the coleopterous genus *Serropalpus* in Leicestershire. *Zoologist* **2**: 701.

WOLLASTON, T.V. (1855). Note on the *Orchesia minor* of British cabinets. *Zoologist* **13**: 4655.

WOLLASTON, T.V. (1857). A revision of the British *Atomariae* with observations on the genus. *Transactions of the entomological Society of London* (New Series) **4**: 64-82.

# *1861 – 1892  Fits and starts*

One entomologist associated with Henry Bates did continue to collect beetles in Leicestershire in the 1860s and 1870s. Harry Holyoak (1906) describes how, as a youngster, he attended Henry Bates' last gypsy party in 1848 before his departure for the Amazon. His father kept a bookshop where Bates and his friends used to meet in the 1840s. After his return from Brazil in 1859, Bates called in at the bookshop and recognised Holyoak with:

*"Why you are the boy we took to Bradgate on that never-to-be-forgotten day!"*.

Holyoak used to visit Bates before the latter moved to London and was persuaded to take up beetles by him. He was already a Lepidopterist and a collecting companion of Frank Plant in Swithland and Buddon Woods. As a Coleopterist, he collected with a Burton-based collector, J. T. Harris, in Leicestershire, the High Peak, Cannock Chase and Coleshill. In 1867 he went to the USA, where he *"wandered about for two years, and spent many pleasant days collecting in the woods and swamps of Delaware and Maryland"*. Holyoak was particularly thrilled to find American species of ground beetles that were closely related to *Calosoma inquisitor*, a British species familiar to him from his excursions to Buddon Wood that climbs trees to feed on caterpillars in the canopy.

However, the golden days of mid-century Leicestershire entomology were now over. According to Holyoak (1906):

*"On my return I found, for a time, no leisure for a hobby, and, moreover, I could not meet with a single kindred spirit in the whole Borough; there seemed to be no person taking the slightest interest in Entomology"*.

Eventually he teamed up with *"a brother collector"* by the splendid name of Mr T. Burbery Forrest. Forrest joined the LLPS on December 15th 1873 and became a council member in 1874. His occupation is not given in the register of members, but that of a Samuel Forrest residing at the same address in Lancaster Place in 1869 is given as *"Gentleman"*. As well as collecting in Leicestershire, Forrest visited the New Forest, Isle of Wight and North Lancashire (Holyoak 1906), but he never published a word and not a single detail survives of any of the species that he caught. Holyoak also knew *"a man named Wilt, a German, who lived at Loughborough, .... a first rate entomologist, having very comprehensive collections of both Lepidoptera and Coleoptera. I often used to visit him, and found him a most interesting acquaintance, as he had done a good deal of collecting in various parts of the world, and had also found time to take part in the Franco-German war"*. Presumably, Wilt is the same man, whom Bouskell (1907) quotes as *"Mr J. Weildt"*, who used to take the Musk beetle, *Aromia moschata*, *"in quantities near Loughborough by putting down fresh dough"*. Weildt is probably responsible for the record of *Aromia moschata* at Loughborough in 1878 attributed by Duffy (1947) to W. Holland, the Reading-based collector and dealer listed by Darby (2006). It is likely that this specimen is still in Holland's collection at Oxford University Museum.

About this time, the LLPS and town museum resumed their joint roles as sponsors of entomological studies. Forrest donated 93 specimens of Leicestershire beetles on September 23rd 1874 and 71 specimens of Leicestershire Chrysomelidae (leaf beetles) on October 17th 1875. In 1876 George Robson "*having been provided with apparatus by the Literary and Philosophical Society,.... made a very interesting collection of the Water Beetles of Leicestershire, which the Society has presented to the Museum, and which are now being mounted for exhibition*" (Anon 1877). The museum was actively trying to develop its entomological collections and in particular a Leicestershire collection for public display. One of the chief motivators for this activity appears to be F.T. Mott, a general naturalist and prominent member of the LLPS (Horwood & Noel 1933). He is referred to by Robson as "*my friend and patron*".

Robson was definitely working class and was often referred to rather patronisingly as an "*artisan naturalist*". According to a museum report (Anon 1876):

"*Mr George Robson* [is] *one of the few of our local artisans who have the wisdom to occupy their spare time in scientific studies*".

Mott (1878) described him as a "*Leicester stocking-maker.... who has found means for self-cultivation while bringing up a large family on the earnings of his frame. There are probably not a dozen men in Leicester of all classes who know as much about the Natural History of their district as he does, and none who love Nature more truly and reverently*".

Robson (1879) published records of 40 water beetle species and seems to have picked up a rather difficult new group quickly in circumstances that were less than ideal. He writes:

"*Hunting the beetles, under the invigorating influences of fresh air and sunshine, was all pleasure; the real work began when I got them home.......... In naming my captures I found the species of Haliplus most difficult to make out, but with the aid of the beautiful microscope belonging to the Leicester Museum, all my difficulties were gradually overcome........The descriptions in Stephens' Manual are so short and vague that no student would be able to get on with that alone*".

By this time, beetles seem to have become less popular among naturalists than in Harley's day. According to Robson (1879):

"*Botany is regarded as a very beautiful science, and Geology has powerful attractions; but beetles! why the very name is too much for the sensitiveness of the ladies and even gentlemen shrink from handling them..........Very little seems to be known by the people generally about the Hydradephaga or Predaceous Water Beetles, in proof of which it may be stated that in all my rambles in search of specimens I never met with any, amongst the mass of those who stopped to look on, who could divine my object*".

Ninety-two specimens of water beetles were lodged in the museum's new Leicestershire collection on June 30th 1877 and he supplied a collection of Staphylinidae (rove beetles) in May 1879. Also in 1879, he published an article in the magazine Science Gossip on mounting and preserving larvae. In the nineteenth century, it was by no means uncommon for working class naturalists to make some money out of the collection or preparation of specimens for other collectors. On September 14th 1878, the LLPS on behalf of the museum purchased 500 specimens of Leicestershire beetles from Mr Oram of Loughborough. Oram may have been connected to a family of butchers who traded under that name in Loughborough (Mary Hider pers. comm.). Later, Oram was paid to prepare spiders, caterpillars and other larvae using a technique that he himself had developed (Anon 1880). It is clear that he was a highly skilled technician at entomological preparations. Could it be that Oram was the "*the working man who was undoubtedly the best hand at mounting beetles that I have met with*" as described by Holyoak (1906)? In support of this theory, Holyoak was introduced to this character by the Loughborough-based Wilt. Holyoak (1906) continues a sad story thus:

"*His work was so beautiful that I was induced to entrust to him the whole of my collection for remounting. Not having heard anything as to the progress of the work for several months, I went over to Loughborough to look him up; but he had disappeared, and no one seemed to know his whereabouts. A few weeks later I saw in the window of a broker's shop in Leicester some of my precious boxes, which I was informed, had been bought at a sale under a distress for rent at Loughborough. My prized insects were in such a frightfully damaged state, and so many of them were altogether missing, that my collecting spirit was completely broken. That was in the year 1878 and from that day ..... I never did another hour's collecting*".

Holyoak published some of his records in two notes in the Entomologist's Monthly Magazine. In 1906 he was invited to give a talk to the LLPS which is published in their Transactions. In it he lists some of his captures from the 1860s and 1870s and provides one of the most valuable sources of information on the history of nineteenth century Leicestershire entomology.

Soon after the demise of Holyoak's collection, work on the museum beetle collections was reported to have made good progress (Anon. 1880), but thereafter was not mentioned and beetle study in the town of Leicester once again seems to have drifted into the doldrums. If any of the museum's Leicestershire beetles added by Forrest, Robson and Oram now survive, they cannot be identified in the current museum collections. In the 1880s, H. E. Quilter, a LLPS member with wide interests, dabbled in beetles and published some observations of *Calosoma inquisitor* and leaf beetles of the genus *Galerucella* and his name appears on the label of a beetle in the museum collections collected in 1908.

Throughout this period, collectors from outside Leicestershire visited Buddon Wood, not only for *Trachodes hispidus* and *Calosoma inquisitor*, but also for the specialities associated with wood ant nests. By this time wood ants appear to have become confined within Leicestershire to Buddon Wood, although in the 1840s they had also been recorded from Sheet Hedges Wood and the Loughborough Outwoods (Plant 1844a). W. G. Blatch from Birmingham collected there in the 1880s and some of his records are listed in his manuscript catalogue of Midland Coleoptera. Canon W. W. Fowler (1887-1891) published Buddon Wood records from Harris and Blatch, and, rather bizarrely, just one species collected by himself. Perhaps he had a bad day.

In general the Leicester-based coleopterists of this period lacked the sustained energy and original enquiry of Henry Bates' generation and far fewer of their records have been handed down to us. But throughout the 1860s, 70s and 80s, the Reverend Andrew Matthews was quietly and independently pursuing his entomological interests in the rural setting of Gumley near Market Harborough. Matthews' father, the Reverend Andrew Hughes Matthews of Weston on the Green, Oxfordshire, was himself an eminent coleopterist who described several British species of the rove beetle genus, *Myllaena*, as new to science. Matthews became rector of Gumley in 1853 and at first occupied himself with birds and Lepidoptera before moving on to beetles (Fowler 1897). The earliest date for any of his beetle records that I have is for *Sphaerius acaroides* taken in 1855 and noted in Frederick Bates' annotations to Sharp's catalogue. His first publication on beetles appeared in the *Zoologist* in 1858 and his first published Leicestershire records appeared in 1860.

*S. acaroides* is a tiny semi-aquatic beetle, 0.7 mm long, which has been found less than half a dozen times in Britain. Its capture illustrates the particular interest of Matthews in small obscure beetles and his proficiency in finding rare species overlooked by the majority of his contemporaries. He became an authority on the *Ptiliidae* (then known as *Trichopterigidae*) or feather-winged beetles not only in Britain, but also worldwide. This family contains the smallest beetle species known to science, British examples ranging from 0.5 mm to 1.2 mm. He described several species collected at Gumley as new to science, although many of these have since been sunk as synonyms of species already known. Some of his species were named after members of his family, such as *Trichopteryx henrici*, named after his brother, and *T. sarae*, named after his wife.

Matthews was a shy man who collected mainly around Gumley, but certainly exchanged specimens with other collectors. According to Fowler (1897):

*"But for his retiring disposition, much more would have been heard of him, but he always preferred to keep himself at home, and very seldom left Gumley, except for a short collecting expedition in Sherwood Forest, or in order to visit some particular friends of similar tastes. He was most generous in helping those younger than himself with knowledge and with specimens."*

It appears that most of Matthews' specimens probably came from Gumley or nearby, but, unfortunately, he was often rather vague about such details. The phrase *"found in this part of the kingdom"* is a typical locality description appearing in his published notes. He seems to have had surprisingly little contact with the Leicester-based naturalists of his day. However, on July 19th 1883 *"a [LLPS] party limited to six members, proceeded by invitation to the residence of the Rev. A. Matthews, Rector of Gumley, who kindly entertained the party, and placed his famous collections of Arthropoda at their disposal, giving them also some most interesting reminiscences of the habits of the rarer species"* (Anon 1884). In 1884, Matthews was reported to have edited *"a list of the Coleoptera of the county worked up by Messrs. Stanyon, Storer and Quilter"* (Anon 1885). Apart from Quilter, mentioned above, there is no other evidence of any expertise of these three LLPS members in the study of beetles, although Stanyon later provided the basis for the Leicestershire list of Heteroptera (plant bugs). They probably based their list on F. Bates' 1854 manuscript catalogue updated from the museum's Leicestershire collection developed in the 1870s. Quilter must have been familiar with Bates' catalogue, because he referred to it in a paper presented to the LLPS (Quilter 1887). In common with many manuscript lists of Leicestershire beetles, the 1884 list was never published and is now lost.

Matthews also supplied a list of Leicestershire beetles to Frederick Bates. Bates wrote in his copy of Sharp's catalogue:

*"In a catalogue of British Coleoptera (by Revs. Fowler and Matthews pub'd in 1883) the Rev. A. Matthews has marked off*

> *(1)      the species that have been found in Leicestershire and*
> *(2)      has given notes etc., on some of the rarer species.*

Bates also transcribed some introductory remarks from Matthews' list:

*"The following list contains the names of the species of Coleoptera which have been found in Leicestershire by my brother and myself since 1855, together with many important additions extracted from an MS catalogue prepared by Mr F. Bates and at present preserved in the Leicester Museum.*

*The species contained in Mr. Bates' catalogue were chiefly obtained from the northern part of the county: whilst our captures were all found in the Market Harborough district on the south-east side of Leicester. The great majority of species are common to both sides of the county. The only species which can be considered at all peculiar or local to Leicestershire are Orchesia minor and Cryphalus abietis.*

*Owing to the absence of wooded or marshland and the high state of cultivation prevalent throughout the south of Leicestershire the entomological fauna is of a very meagre description when compared with the other parts of the Kingdom and the rarer insects which have occurred are generally represented by single or at the most 3 or 4 examples."*

Matthews' records are clearly marked in Bates' annotations and constitute the first Leicestershire records for large numbers of species in some of the more difficult families such as the Staphylinidae (rove beetles). Matthews' description of his list as containing few rarities is completely at odds with the contents of his list, which contained many rare species and several with coastal or other habitats unrepresented in Leicestershire. Next to a few of these, Bates wrote *"I doubt these being Leicestershire"*. Some of Matthews' records of rarities are undoubtedly correct. A voucher specimen for his record of the water beetle, *Hydrochus brevis*, survives in the remnants of his collection at Bolton Museum. It is actually a recently described species, *H. megaphallus*, but Matthews' identification was sound according to taxonomic knowledge at that time. His record of the water beetle, *Berosus signaticollis*, is substantiated by its rediscovery over one hundred years later at Saddington Reservoir, less than two miles from Gumley. However, records of coastal species such as the ground beetle, *Dicheirotrichus gustavi*, or the flea beetle, *Chaetocnema sahlbergi*, must be viewed as unreliable. Consequently, it is difficult to accept Matthews' records unless they are corroborated by other data in some way. Some of the more doubtful records were filtered out of later Leicestershire lists, but others keep reappearing in works summarising vice county distributions and as isolated dots in modern distribution maps.

It is unclear how so many false records were introduced into the work of someone who displayed considerable skill in finding and identifying species from difficult groups. Identification problems can be largely discounted because many of the more extraordinary species listed are quite distinctive. The lack of locality labels on Matthews' specimens, coupled with the failing memory of an elderly gentleman may be one possible explanation. Alternatively, a list of species in his collection may have been misinterpreted as a Leicestershire list. We shall probably never know.

Map of Leicestershire and Rutland showing main localities mentioned in the text

LOUGHBOROUGH

Buddon Wood

Bardon Hill

CHARNWOOD FOREST

Bradgate Park

RUTLAND

Oakham

Owston Wood

Barrowden

Market Bosworth

Leicester

Shenton Hall

Earl Shilton

Kibworth

Uppingham

Saddington Reservoir

Gumley

VALE OF BELVOIR

A scene in Bradgate Park drawn by John Martin in 1842 at around the time that Henry Walter Bates first studied beetles there

ADVENTURE WITH CURL-CRESTED TOUCANS.

Frontispiece to Vol. I.

Frontispiece from Bates' *The Naturalist on the River Amazons* depicting an adventure on one of the author's intrepid collecting trips in Brazil

Donisthorpe at the 'BM'

Henry Walter Bates as a young man

S.O. Taylor in the uniform of the wartime civil
defence corps

Frank Bouskell in 1907, clubbable social secretary
and compiler of the only published list of
Leicestershire beetles

Claude Henderson and Don Tozer out in the field in Majorca

# Coleopterists active in Leicestershire 1860 to 1892

| Name | Born | Died | Active in Leics | Main biographic sources |
|------|------|------|-----------------|-------------------------|
| William Gabriel Blatch | 1840 | 25.2.1900 | 1882-1884 | Fowler (1900) |
| T. Burberry Forrest | ? | ? | 1874-1875 | Holyoak (1906), LLPS & Museum sources |
| William Weekes Fowler | 1.1849 | 3.6.1923 | 1880s? | Walker (1923) |
| John Thomas Harris | c1830 | 3.10.1892 | 1860-1865 | Fowler (1892), Holyoak (1906) |
| Harry Holyoak | 1844 | ? | c1860-1878 | Holyoak (1906) |
| Andrew Matthews | 18.6.1815 | 14.9.1897 | 1855-c1889 | Fowler (1897) |
| Oram | ? | ? | 1878 | Museum records |
| H.E. Quilter | c1850 | 1915 | 1884-1886, 1908 | LLPS sources, Horwood & Noel (1933) |
| George Robson | ? | ? | 1876-1879 | Mott (1878), Museum records |
| J. Weildt/Wilt | ? | ? | 1870s | Holyoak (1906), Bouskell (1907) |

# Manuscript sources for the period 1860 to 1892

W.G. Blatch's Catalogue of Midland Coleoptera (Manchester Museum)
Leicester Museum Accessions Ledger (Leicester City Museums Service)
LLPS Register of Members (Leics Record Office - 14D55/30)
Frederick Bates' annotations of Sharp's catalogue (C. MacKechnie Jarvis)

# Main Literature sources for Leicestershire beetle records 1860 to 1892

CROTCH, G.R. (1896). Revision of the catalogue of British Coleoptera. *Entomologist* **31**: 111.

FOWLER, W.W. (1885). Notes on British Coleoptera since 1871 with notices of doubtful species and of others that require to be omitted from the British list. *Entomologist's monthly Magazine* **19**: 200.

FOWLER, W.W. (1885). The Nitidulidae of Great Britain. *Entomologist's monthly Magazine* **22**: 76.

FOWLER, W.W. (1887-1891). *The Coleoptera of the British Islands.* (5 volumes) London: L. Reeve & Co.

FOWLER, W.W. (1889). On the British species of the genus *Anaspis* with description of a new species. *Entomologist's monthly Magazine* **25**: 331-338.

HOLYOAK, H. (1865). Capture of *Trachodes hispidus*. *Entomologist's monthly Magazine* **2**: 87.

HOLYOAK, H. (1871). Captures of Coleoptera in Buddon Wood, Leicestershire. *Entomologist's monthly Magazine* **8**: 85-86.

MACAULEY, T. & BROWNE, M. (1885). *Report of the Council of the Leicester Literary and Philosophical Society presented to the Annual General Meeting, June 22nd 1885.* Leicester.

MATTHEWS, A. (1860). Notes on the British Trichopterygidae with description of some new species. *Zoologist* **18**: 7063-7068.

MATTHEWS, A. (1862). Capture of *Cryphalus abietis* and *Cryphalus piceae* near Market Harborough. *Zoologist* **20**: 7918.

MATTHEWS, A. (1862). Capture of *Scydmaenus godarti* and other Coleoptera new to the British fauna. *Zoologist* **20**: 7975-7976.

MATTHEWS, A. (1862). Capture of *Antherophagus silaceus* Herbst, *Agathidium rotundatum* Gyll. and other Coleoptera. *Zoologist* **20**: 8084.

MATTHEWS, A. (1863). Capture of *Ptilium affine, Omalium nigrum, O. brevicorne, O. testaceum*, and a new species of *Omalium*. *Zoologist* **21**: 8649-8652.

MATTHEWS, A. (1865). On various species of *Trichopterygidae* new to Britain. *Entomologist's monthly Magazine* **1**: 173-178.

MATTHEWS, A. (1865). Notes on some species of *Trichopterygidae* new to Britain and of various alterations of nomenclature in the same family. *Entomologist's monthly Magazine* **2**: 241-245.

MATTHEWS, A. (1871). New British Trichopterygidae (with diagnoses of new species). *Entomologist's monthly Magazine* **8**: 151-152.

MATTHEWS, A. (1878). Descriptions of two new species of Trichopteryx and record of the capture of *T. volans* in Britain. *Entomologist's monthly Magazine* **15**: 64-65.

MATTHEWS, A. (1885). Synopses of the British species of *Orthoperus*. *Entomologist's monthly Magazine* **22**: 107-110.

MATTHEWS, A. (1889). New genera and species of Trichopterygidae. *Annals and Magazine of Natural History (6)* **3**: 188-195.

QUILTER, H.E. (1887). The metamorphoses of *Galeruca nymphea* Lin. *Transactions of the Leicester Literary and Philosophical Society* **1**: 17-20.

ROBSON, G. (1879). The predaceous water beetles (Hydradephaga) of Leicestershire. *Midland Naturalist* **2**: 57-60.

RYE, E.C. (1863). New British species, corrections of nomenclature etc. noticed since the publication of the Entomologist's Annual, 1861. *Entomologist's Annual* **1863**: 65-115.

SHARP, D. (1871). Notes on Dr Sharp's catalogue of British Coleoptera. *Entomologist's monthly Magazine* **8**: 83-84.

WOLLASTON, T.V. (1872). Capture of a *Scymnus* new to Britain. *Entomologist's monthly Magazine* **9**: 117.

# 1893 – 1907  Bouskell and friends

The study of Leicestershire beetles had limped along for decades with few signs of any sustained activity, so it comes as a surprise when suddenly we read of the Leicester Entomological Club in 1893 with F. Bates Esq. in the chair and the Hon. Sec. reporting on its Easter excursion to Charnwood Forest (Bouskell 1893). Numerous records of Coleoptera and Lepidoptera are listed and they are but the first of a series of published records from the Charnwood Forest and Owston Woods to appear during the 1890s. At first most of the beetle records probably emanated from Frederick Bates culminating in an extensive list of 507 beetle species from Bradgate Park (Bates, F. 1896). However, two young entomologists in their twenties, who at first concentrated on the Lepidoptera, later graduated onto beetles: Frank Bouskell and C.B. Headly.

On January 25th 1894, the twelve members of the Leicester Entomological Club reconstituted themselves as Section F (entomology) of the Leicester Literary and Philosophical Society (LLPS) (Anon 1894) and thereafter the membership steadily increased until by April 1899 it had reached 56. The moving organisational force behind much of this activity was the long term secretary, Frank Bouskell. In the Entomological Record published in London we read that "t*he Leicester Society (under the able presidency of Mr. F. Rowley, and the enthusiastic secretary, Mr. F. Bouskell) is doing excellent work.*" (Anon 1898). In the same report on a society dinner, we read that:

"*At the speech-making after the dinner, Mr. Dixon bore remarkable testament to the excellence of the secretary. He said: "Mr. Bouskell does not ask one to do so and so, but writes 'You are down to do so and so,' and thus you have to do it. Here's a secretary after our own heart."*

The society held monthly indoor evening meetings between October and June and organised three or four local excursions a year as well as an annual four day trip to the New Forest at Whitsun and an annual weekend in August at Wicken Fen in Cambridgeshire. In 1895, the society put on the first of several conversazione, which was attended by 150 people. An entomological exhibition of all the specimens shown at the *conversazione* was opened the next day and attracted 250 members of the public (Vice 1896). On 13th January 1897 the first of a series of annual dinners was held (Anon 1897).

All these activities attracted members from outside Leicestershire and it is evident that the society quickly established a reputation for conviviality:

"*Like all societies that do not wish to fall into a midway condition, this society combines the social with the scientific. The result must be very gratifying to the officers and certainly repays them for the extra trouble. Professor Beare, and Messrs. Donisthorpe and Tutt, were the London members present at the latest social function on January 13th, and to say that these gentlemen have taken away an excellent impression of the generous hospitality of their Midland friends is to put the matter very mildly.*" (Anon 1898).

In 1894, Bertram Rye participated in an excursion to Bardon Hill and published the results in the Entomologist's monthly magazine (Rye & Skinner 1895). However, it was Donisthorpe who both contributed and benefited most through his association with the Leicester society. Donisthorpe was born in Leicestershire at Earl Shilton, but lived in Kensington for much of his life.

In 1879, he collected his first beetle at nine years old while still living at Earl Shilton. He was the same age as Bouskell and there seems to be a reference in Donisthorpe's journal to a joint collecting trip to Groby Pool in 1885 when they were both fifteen years old. From 1897 he went on many collecting expeditions with him, at first in Leicestershire and on society excursions to the New Forest, and later further afield to places such as South Kerry in Ireland. In his contribution to Donisthorpe's obituary, Bouskell (1951) described him as "*my oldest friend.*" Donisthorpe published a series of papers in the Transactions of the Leicester Literary and Philosophical Society and his Leicestershire trips were an important stage in the development of his burgeoning entomological career. It was at Buddon Wood that he first became interested in beetles associated with ant nests. He later went on to write the definitive book on the guests of British ants (Donisthorpe 1927). He became a leading figure in the study of British beetles throughout the first half of the twentieth century.

Donisthorpe was unarguably a colourful character. He was born into money and appears to have never done a stroke of paid work in his life. However, he was extremely diligent in his insect studies. He made important contributions to our knowledge of the beetle fauna of Windsor Park, published around 800 books, papers and notes including an update to the standard work on British beetles (Fowler & Donisthorpe 1913) and described numerous new species and varieties in the British beetle fauna. His trigger happy approach to describing new species was not always appreciated by his contemporaries:

"*While there is no doubt but that 'Donnie' as he was known to his friends, had an unusually keen eye for a new species, about 30 having been described by him on the British list, not to mention numerous new varieties of already known species and known continental species first discovered in Britain by him, his zeal sometimes led him into indiscretion and some of his new species will have to be abandoned as insufficiently distinct*" (Blair 1951).

His eccentricities were not confined to an enthusiasm for naming new species:

"*Mr. Donisthorpe was a very fine coleopterist, but he had that curious 'kink' shared by one or two other people, that he would only put in his collection beetles he had taken with his own hands. Luckily for him he was a man of leisure and was able to go about the country when he heard of any rare beetles being taken. It led, however, to some curious results, as on a celebrated occasion when a collector in the New Forest got a very rare beetle and advised Mr. Donisthorpe, who telegraphed him to put a tumbler over it on the ground and keep it there until he was able to go and collect it himself.*" (Lloyd 1951)

Perhaps less eccentric was his eye for the ladies. His collecting companion, Miss Florence Kirk is frequently mentioned in his entomological notes. Less well publicised is the story, still circulating by oral tradition, of his being thrown into a ditch by a morally indignant warden of Wicken Fen after being surprised in a compromising situation. On his last visit to Leicestershire in 1941, he was accompanied around Gopsall Park by his cousin, Mrs Primrose Griffiths (Donisthorpe 1941). Amongst his captures was a species that he decided was new to science. He named it, *Cerylon primrosae*, after his charming host. Needless to say, notwithstanding the charms of Mrs Griffiths, this species has since been sunk as identical to the widespread and common *C. ferrugineus*. However, it is a testament to his collecting abilities that he also took on that day a rove beetle, *Phloeodroma concolor* (now *Phloeopora concolor*) that had never been recorded previously in Britain nor since.

Several locally based coleopterists were operating in the 1890s. In November 1896, soon after publishing his epic work on Bradgate Park, Frederick Bates moved away to Chiswick, but by then the baton had been taken up by the next generation. Charles Burnard Headly (also spelt Headley) was born in 1868 into a family that owned an ironmonger's business. His initials are sometimes shortened to BH, but Burnard was his mother's family name, so I doubt that it was used as his Christian name. An analysis of the dates on labels in his collection suggests that Headly collected his first beetle in 1890, but did not get into his stride until 1893 (Brind 1980). He accompanied Bates to Bradgate Park, who reported that *"Mr Headly joined me for several weeks and collected most assiduously."* He also gave several joint presentations with Bouskell to the entomology section of the LLPS, the first being on *"The onion grub"* given on 27th February 1894. Judging by the localities on his collection labels, much of his collecting was done in Charnwood and the New Forest on entomological section excursions, but he also ventured out to the south east of the city (several beetles come from Stoughton) and to Devon and Cornwall, where his mother's family originated. In 1897 he collected several stored product species from the city of Leicester (Bouskell 1898). In the 1901 census, he gave his occupation as 'naturalist'. At that time he was working as an assistant in the town museum, but it seems likely that he was doing it for interest rather than as a living.

James H Woolley (also spelt Wooley) was a gardener and bailiff who lived in Leicester Frith, a civil parish containing only half a dozen households and located more or less where County Hall now stands at Glenfield. This is not far from Bradgate and Bates (1896) reported that *"I have received from Mr. J.H. Woolley a list of species obtained from Sphagnum got out of the park"*. Woolley published several notes on Coleoptera around Leicester Frith, including a piece on beetles attacking strawberries (Woolley 1895a). He did not join the section until 1896 and he probably did not move in the same social circles as Bouskell, Headly and Donisthorpe, who were all confirmed bachelors, while Woolley was married with a family. He was over ten years older than the others. Conflicting birth dates are given in various censuses, but he was probably born between 1856 and 1858. There were also differences in social class, illustrated perhaps by the fact that Woolley was not on the guest list for the 1905 section dinner. Nevertheless, he obviously participated fully in the entomological activity of the section. On the 10th December 1897 he presented a paper on a review of the British Carabidae with special reference to Leicestershire species. In one of his published notes he describes the results of collecting in November, outside the main collecting season

*"There is not a month in the year that may not be productive of fresh and often good species to the diligent beetle collector. The best time for securing the many species that take shelter under loose bark is during cold weather in winter, at which time they are by no means lively, hence they are easily secured. I always get the best results from old beech trees in which the bark cracks up into medium sized, close lying scales, which afford good shelter for small insects: and after autumn rain these scales are easily pulled off even with the fingers. But an old, dead, half decayed, recently felled beech tree is sure to provide a store house of good things to the Coleopterist, a boon which seldom falls to his lot, but which is calculated to produce sensations better realised than described."* (Woolley 1895b)

The Rev. Canon C.T. Crutwell was an original member of the Leicester Entomological Club. He appears to have been primarily a Lepidopterist and published no records of beetles during his time in Leicestershire, but he was credited by Bouskell (1907) with working on Leicestershire beetles and his small beetle collection survives him. Fowler (1911) reports his finding of a rare ground beetle, *Amara alpina*, on top of a Scottish mountain.

According to Dixey (1911), "*Crutwell was a man of varied interests and activities. Nothing in the world of intellect seemed to come amiss to him.*" As well as excelling as an athlete in his youth, he had followed a brilliant academic career at Oxford in the classics and Hebrew before making a fateful decision to change the course of his life:

"*His extreme sense of duty led* [Crutwell] *in 1877 to resign his position in* [Merton]*College in favour of a post , where, as he thought, he could exercise more influence over the lives of his pupils by catching them at a comparatively early stage of their mental development. But his career as Headmaster, first of Bradfield and afterwards of Malvern was not in every respect a success. He was probably too sensitive and conscientious to be thoroughly comfortable amid the worries and anxieties inseparable from the conduct of a great school; and when he left Malvern in 1885, it was plain that the strain of the last few years had told on him severely. The remainder of his life was passed in the more congenial surroundings of country parishes, varied by his terms of residence as Canon of Peterborough.*" Dixey (1911)

It is possible that Crutwell was responsible for several unattributed records from Kibworth, where he was curate until 1901. However, another, otherwise unknown collector, a Miss M.E. Whitton, was also credited with records of beetles from Kibworth by Bouskell (1901) and Donisthorpe. A Miss Arkwright is occasionally mentioned in LLPS reports and in 1898 she presented a collection of beetles to the museum, some of which can still be identified today, albeit without locality labels. W. Moss of Loughborough is another enigmatic figure, who exhibited beetles from Loughborough Meadow to the section in 1894. He afterwards dropped off the list of members and was never heard of again.

As well as organising the entomology section, Bouskell found time to collect beetles and published an extensive account of his activities in 1897 (Bouskell 1898). In 1897 or 1898 he moved to Market Bosworth to practise as a solicitor, but he still continued to play a leading role in the entomology section and collect beetles. In 1901 he published a lengthy paper on British dung beetles (Bouskell 1901). In 1903 he published the discovery of an exotic longhorn beetle new to Britain from Market Bosworth (Bouskell 1903a). However, with the exception of Frederick Bates, it is not the collecting acumen of Bouskell and his Leicestershire contemporaries that best mark out their entomological achievements. Outside of the immediate area where they lived, their Leicestershire excursions were confined to repeated visits to the same honey-pot sites and although they added significantly to the species known from the county, their collecting activity was not sustained long enough for them to develop an expertise in difficult groups or in finding particularly rare species. Bouskell's major contribution to the knowledge of Leicestershire beetles arose out of his energy and organisational capabilities which provided a platform for others to flourish and for their collected records to be published for posterity. His first major success was the reawakening of Frederick Bates' interest in local beetles and the publication of Bates' immensely valuable paper on the beetles of Bradgate Park. In 1901, Bouskell was asked to prepare a list of Leicestershire beetles in preparation for the visit of the British Association for the Advancement of Science, which eventually took place in 1907 (Anon 1907). The list was published as part of the Victoria County History (Bouskell 1907). It has many gaps represented by common species that were presumably meant to be taken as read and considered too uninteresting to enumerate. Unfortunately, the main manuscript on which it was based has been lost together with previous lists by Matthews and Bates that provided a foundation. This loss probably happened during a house fire at Bouskell's home. However, some of the gaps in the published list can be filled from the Bates annotated checklist, already mentioned.

In addition, Professor Balfour-Browne, the renowned water beetle specialist transcribed the water beetle records onto a card index, now held by the Scottish National Museum. Whatever its shortcomings, Bouskell's list remains the only published list of Leicestershire beetles. From 1854 to the present day, one comes across numerous references to committees and sub-committees charged with the production of Leicestershire lists, but Bouskell is the only person to have actually completed his task.

The beetle fauna of Rutland remained almost unknown at this time. The paltry list of beetles in the Victoria County History of Rutland (Douglas 1908) is based on the observations of schoolboys in the Uppingham School Natural Science Society that were published in the society's report for 1900. Examination of the original source reveals that some of the records, on which the Rutland list is based, actually came from Northamptonshire. The reliability of the identifications is difficult to assess and there is at least one transcription error resulting in the false listing of *Amara fulva*, a rather rare ground beetle, otherwise unrecorded in Rutland.

The flowering of Leicestershire beetle study in the 1890s was bright but brief. Headly gave no talks to the entomology section after 1895, although he continued attending the New Forest excursions until 1899 and remained an intermittent member up until 1910. He collected his last beetle in 1906 and donated his collection to the Leicester Museum in 1909. By this time his interests had moved to photography, microscopy and then botany (Horwood & Noel 1933), but he eventually lost contact with the world of natural history altogether and the date of his death remains unknown and unmarked by any obituary or notice. Woolley remained an active member of the entomology section for twenty-three years, but he appears to have ceased generating published beetle records after 1898. His occasional talks to the section centred on horticultural pests from 1899 onward, although in 1915 he intriguingly gave a presentation on Coleoptera from Vancouver. He probably died some time before 30th March 1942, when his collection was incorporated into that of another local coleopterist. Bouskell continued to collect beetles, often in company with Donisthorpe until at least 1909. The coleopterists who started in the 1920s did not know him, so he had probably stopped collecting before then. For the rest of his life he concentrated his energies on gardening and horticultural shows, but still retained his organisational drive. From 1920 to 1921 he was chairman of the Market Bosworth Show and Country Sports Fair and he was often called upon to judge in horticultural shows at Shrewsbury, Edinburgh and Chelsea. He was a governor both at the local grammar and secondary modern schools and was elected to the County Council in 1922, where he became alderman in 1937 and served on the Leicestershire and Rutland police authority. When I gave a talk to the Market Bosworth Natural History Society in the early 1990s, one of the audience could still remember him. He eventually passed away peacefully on 1st February 1952:

*"Ald. Frank Bouskell, the Market Bosworth solicitor, who brought an old-world fragrance to the profession of the law by invariably wearing a buttonhole flower, died at his Bosworth home yesterday aged 82. With him passed a tradition of Victorian gentility he had preserved for more than half a century. Only a few days ago, a silvery-haired figure, he was busy at this office overlooking Bosworth square. He walked through the frost-bound garden of his home at Sedgemere and inspected the huge, frozen lily pond, where the aquatic plants were embalmed in ice. An intimate friend who saw him in his last few days said that his life was ended by no definite illness. He merely reached the end of his season."* (Anon 1952)

The entomology section went into a slow terminal decline after the turn of the century. Two further coleopterists, Dr. W.H. Barrow and S.O. Taylor became members in the first decade of the next century, but their influence did not really begin until the next phase of Leicestershire activity. In 1905 we read that:

*"The entomological Society of Leicester, after an unexpected period of aestivation, following its brilliant spring-like entry into existence a few years ago, has reawakened once more into active existence."* (Anon 1905)

This passage of praise from London was prompted by the re-establishment of the annual dinner, but any renaissance was short lived. In the same year, Bouskell handed over as honorary secretary of the entomology section after fourteen active years in the post. He remained the position of chairman or vice-chairman until 1912, but we read that on 18th June 1908:

*"An excursion had been arranged to Sherwood Forest, but only two members put in an appearance, and they reluctantly abandoned the trip."* (Whittingham 1908)

By 1915 the membership was back to twelve, the same number that had started in 1894. The section was finally suspended in 1920.

# Coleopterists active in Leicestershire 1893 to 1907

| *Name* | *Born* | *Died* | *Active in Leics* | *Main biographic sources* |
| --- | --- | --- | --- | --- |
| Frederick Bates | 28.11.1829 | 6.10.1903 | 1848-1896 | Donisthorpe (1903) |
| T Hudson Beare | | | 1897 | |
| Frank Bouskell | 1870 | 1.2.1952 | 1885-1909 | Reports of section F published in LLPS Transactions |
| Charles Thomas Crutwell | 1847 | 4.4.1911 | 1892-1895 | Dixey (1911), Fowler (1911) |
| Horace St. John Kelly Donisthorpe | 17.3.1870 | 22.4.1951 | 1879-1941 | Blair (1951), Bouskell (1951), Lloyd (1951) |
| Charles Burnard Headly | 1868 | ? | 1891-1900 | Brind (1980), Horwood & Noel (1933), Reports of section F published in LLPS Transactions |
| W. Moss | ? | ? | 1893-1894 | Reports of section F published in LLPS Transactions |
| Bertram G. Rye | 24.9.1872 | 7.11.1939 | 1894 | Anon. (1969) |
| M.E. Whitton (Miss) | ? | ? | from before 1901 | Bouskell (1901), Fowler & Donisthorpe (1913) |
| J.H. Woolley | c1856-1858 | c1942? | 1894-1898 | Reports of section F published in LLPS Transactions |

# Manuscript sources for the period 1893 to 1907

Frederick Bates' annotations of Sharp's catalogue (C. MacKechnie Jarvis)
W.A.F. Balfour Browne's card index (National Museum of Scotland)
H.St.J.K. Donisthorpe's Collection Catalogue (Natural History Museum, London)

# Main literature sources for Leicestershire beetle records 1893 to 1907

ANON. (1894). Report on Societies. *Entomologist's record* **5**: 136.

BATES, F. (1896). The Coleoptera of Bradgate Park. *Transactions of the Leicester Literary and Philosophical Society* **4**: 170-176.

BOUSKELL, F. (1894). Leicester Entomological Club. *Entomologist's record* **4**: 163-164.

BOUSKELL, F. (1898). Leicestershire Coleoptera in 1897. *Entomologist's record* **10**: 19-22.

BOUSKELL, F. (1901). The Variation and Distribution of the genus *Aphodius* (Illiger). *Transactions of the Leicester Literary and Philosophical Society* **5**: 571-605.

BOUSKELL, F. (1901). Reports of the Sections: Section "F" for Entomology. *Transactions of the Leicester Literary and Philosophical Society* **5**: 700-703.

BOUSKELL, F. (1901). Reports of the Sections: Section "F" Entomology. *Transactions of the Leicester Literary and Philosophical Society* **6**: 96-97.

BOUSKELL, F. (1903). *Tetropium castaneum* L.- a species of Longicorn Coleoptera new to Britain. *Entomologist's record* **15**: 288.

BOUSKELL, F. (1903). Reports of the Sections: Section "F" Entomology. *Transactions of the Leicester Literary and Philosophical Society* **7**: 202.

BOUSKELL, F. (1904). Reports of the Sections: Section "F" Entomology. *Transactions of the Leicester Literary and Philosophical Society* **8**: 84-87.

BOUSKELL, F. (1904). Reports of the Sections: Section "F" Entomology. *Transactions of the Leicester Literary and Philosophical Society* **8**: 151-153.

BOUSKELL, F. (1907). Insects in PAGE, W. (ed.), *The Victoria History of the County of Rutland 1.* London: Archibald Constable pp 64-94.

DIXON, G.B. (1905). Quarterly Reports of the Sections: Section F for Entomology. *Transactions of the Leicester Literary and Philosophical Society* **9**: 81-90.

DONISTHORPE, H.St.J. (1898). Notes on the British *Longicornes*. *Transactions of the Leicester Literary and Philosophical Society* **5**: 25-37.

DONISTHORPE, H.St.J. (1901). On the Origin of, and Progress in the Study of Myrmecophilous Coleoptera. *Transactions of the Leicester Literary and Philosophical Society* **6**: 16-28.

DONISTHORPE, H.St.J. (1902). *Dorcatoma chrysomelina* etc. in Leicestershire. *Entomologist's Record* **14**: 267.

DONISTHORPE, H.St.J. (1905). Coleoptera at Market Bosworth. *Entomologist's Record* **17**: 18.

DOUGLAS, R.N. (1908). Insects in PAGE, W. (ed.), *The Victoria History of the County of Leicester* **1**. London: Archibald Constable pp 39-45.

FOWLER, W.W. & DONISTHORPE, H.StJ.K. (1913). *The Coleoptera of the British Islands.* (volume 6) London: L. Reeve & Co.

ROWLEY, F.R. (1898). Quarterly Reports of the Sections: Section F for Entomology. *Transactions of the Leicester Literary and Philosophical Society* **5**: 84.

RYE, B.G. & SKINNER, P.F. (1894). Coleoptera in 1894. *Entomologist's monthly Magazine* **30**: 276-277.

VICE, W.A. (1894). Quarterly Reports of the Sections: Section F for Entomology. *Transactions of the Leicester Literary and Philosophical Society* **3**: 377-380.

VICE, W.A. (1895). Quarterly Reports of the Sections: Section F for Entomology. *Transactions of the Leicester Literary and Philosophical Society* **3**: 447-450.

VICE, W.A. (1895). Quarterly Reports of the Sections: Section F for Entomology. *Transactions of the Leicester Literary and Philosophical Society* **4**: 28-31.

VICE, W.A. (1896). Quarterly Reports of the Sections: Section F for Entomology. *Transactions of the Leicester Literary and Philosophical Society* **4**: 85-92.

VICE, W.A. (1896). Quarterly Reports of the Sections: Section F for Entomology. *Transactions of the Leicester Literary and Philosophical Society* **4**: 197-202.

WOOLLEY, J.H. (1895). Beetle collecting in November. *Naturalist's Journal Magazine* **4**: 43.

WOOLLEY, J.H. (1895). Coleoptera at Leicester. *Naturalist's Journal Magazine* **4**: 141.

WOOLLEY, J.H. (1895). Strawberries, beetles and hedgehogs. *Naturalist's Journal Magazine* **4**: 251-252.

# *1908 – 1959  The age of collectors*

Unlike in the previous century, there were no clean breaks in activity during the twentieth century and each period overlaps with the previous, even if it is subtly different in character. Consequently, 1907 is a rather arbitrary date of transition chosen primarily to mark the publication of the Leicestershire list in the Victoria County History. In fact, Dr. W. H. Barrow, the first of the next generation of Leicestershire coleopterists appears in the reports of the entomology section of the LLPS as early as 1902, when he *"gave a fine exhibition of microscope slides illustrating various points in the anatomy of the order Coleoptera"* (Bouskell 1903b). In 1904 he presented a paper to the entomology section entitled *"A retrospect of a season's collecting"* (Barrow 1905). Also in 1904, the section enjoyed a talk by a second new face, S.O. Taylor, who *"read an interesting paper on the Coleoptera found in his house and garden in Leicester"* (Dixon 1905). They both subsequently played active roles in the section, both as officers and speakers at evening meetings. To call them the next generation, however, is something of a misnomer. In the 1901 census Barrow's age was given as 44, while Taylor's was given as 31, so Barrow was considerably older than Bouskell, while Taylor was the same age. Both started their interest in beetles relatively late. Taylor's collection notebook shows that he started his collection in 1903, when he was 32 years old. However, while Bouskell and Headly gave up beetles and moved on to other things, Barrow and Taylor actively continued their interest into old age.

Dr. Barrow, as he was usually referred to, was a doctor of music and his occupation is listed as music teacher in the 1901 census. He should not be confused with W. Hubert Barrow, the slightly later Leicester Museum taxidermist and wheeler-dealer of bird skins[2]. Dr. Barrow is linked to Taylor through their professions. Taylor's occupation is listed as organ builder in the 1901 census and his work entailed the maintenance of church organs. In 1984 I visited W. Hunt in Barnstaple, Devon, also a music teacher and coleopterist, who had grown up in a musical family in Sutton in the Elms, Leicestershire. Hunt was born around 1893 and he knew Taylor and Dr Barrow when he was a boy. In conversation, he described how Taylor and Dr. Barrow would take a train to Sutton in the Elms on Thursdays and visit his father for a drink (Lott 1984). Hunt would then accompany them on a collecting trip. In a nice tie up, Barrow published a note on the capture of a rare rove beetle from haystack refuse at Sutton in the Elms in 1912 (Barrow 1912).

In 1922 the ranks of the Leicestershire coleopterists were swelled by two new schoolboy recruits. Claude Henderson and Don Tozer grew up in the same neighbourhood of Leicester and shared an interest in collecting butterflies and moths. One day they went to Leicester Museum to see the insect collections on display in the public gallery, where they met S.O. Taylor, who was curating the beetle collections (Evans 1983). Taylor persuaded them both to take up beetles. Tozer described Taylor as *"always ready to help"* and he used to take specimens round to Taylor's house for help with identification. Henderson and Tozer were close friends and went on collecting holidays together, even after Henderson got married. Over the next three decades several other local naturalists developed an interest in beetles. Ken Clark, another boyhood friend of Henderson and Tozer went out collecting with them.

---

[2] Just to make matters even more confusing, there is another H.W. Barrow, whose name appears in Don Tozer's collection on several specimens of the Great Silver Water Beetle, *Hydrophilus piceus*, dating from the early thirties. The beetles were found at Barrow Brothers' Brickyard on Barkby Thorpe Lane. Tozer once told me a story of a complete beginner, who tried his luck in a pond with a child's net designed for the beach and came up with the Great Silver Water Beetle, the largest British water beetle and a great rarity for Leicestershire.

R. Woodward occasionally went collecting with Tozer, who told me that he was a policeman. Tozer also knew W. Turner, whose exchange specimens turn up occasionally in other collections, and J.K. Bates, who lived in Barrowden in Rutland and had a general interest in natural history. Bates collected around 200 beetles in the forties and fifties. A couple of his records of other insect groups are quoted in the entomological press (Smith & Bates 1956, Scudder 1957). Unlike the others, he was a university graduate, having studied zoology at Durham and carried out research on fleas at Oxford. He died tragically by suicide in 1957. Other collectors undoubtedly operated in the area during this time. T.W. Tailby was a teacher living in Church Langton, then Kibworth. He had wide-ranging interests in natural history that included beetles. He does not appear to have exchanged specimens with Tozer and the other Leicestershire collectors, but he did incorporate large numbers of Headly and Taylor specimens into his own collections from the museum. I have little doubt that this was done with the agreement of museum curators, who probably imagined that they were encouraging the study of Leicestershire beetles. If this practice was followed with other naturalists, it could explain why so many of the older specimens have been lost from the museum collections. A few years after his death, some members of Tailby's family came into the museum to see his collections. Tailby had told them that he had given one of his incomplete beetles a wooden leg and they asked specifically to see it, a request that caused the museum staff some not inconsiderable problems.

The main goal for most of these coleopterists was the building of a comprehensive collection of British beetles. To this end, they regularly exchanged specimens both among themselves and with fellow collectors from around the country. Their specimens are tidily mounted on card attached to a pin and, apart from Barrow's collection, labelled with date and locality of capture. In most cases the details are written on the underside of the card, but in Henderson's collection they are written on a separate label in beautiful handwriting and the specimens arranged in drawers in perfectly neat rows. The high standard of specimen preparation was achieved through a laborious process. After capture, the beetles were despatched in a killing jar using amyl acetate or hydrogen cyanide from laurel leaves. The beetles would then be quickly rough-mounted by gluing them onto ordinary card, before they dried out and became too brittle. Gum tragacanth, a water-soluble glue used in cake decorations, was recommended in the standard guidance published in books and magazines, but Tozer told me that he just used ordinary paper glue from Woolworth shops. The specimens were later floated off their rough mounts, relaxed if necessary, and remounted on good quality card by carefully arranging their legs and antennae into standard positions. The results are a perfect reference collection for comparing different specimens when identifying species or looking for characteristic morphological features.

The twentieth century Leicestershire collectors belonged to a nationwide group of people, overwhelmingly male, who developed a devouring interest in a particular hobby. They benefited from the widely available education from late Victorian times onward and usually followed occupations that required skills and responsibility, even if they were not high-powered. Henderson was a laboratory technician at Loughborough Technical College. Tozer joined his father as a painter and decorator. Clark qualified as a chartered mechanical engineer after joining the British United Shoe Machinery Company as an apprentice straight from school. They shared with stamp-collectors and train-spotters an instinctive urge to collect and complete series and a brain that embraced classification and lists, but like birdwatchers and amateur archaeologists they applied their minds to aspects of their surroundings that gave them a privileged insight into the intricacies of the world in which we all live. Their knowledge of the natural world was profound, because to be successful fin inding rare beetles, they needed an understanding of botany, ecology, geomorphology and landscape history. It is no accident that many of them had wider interests. Henderson was an amateur astronomer, a keen gardener and a passionate photographer of wild orchids throughout Britain and beyond. Clark was a keen cyclist (both touring and competition) and motor-cyclist. As well as building and maintaining organs professionally, Taylor made cellos and was an accomplished musician.

The best way of obtaining perfect specimens for a collection is to keep breeding pairs and rear the larvae through to adults, so this is what they did and in doing so, they discovered the life histories of many species. Spare progeny were often released into the garden, but this sometimes produced unexpected results:

"[Don Tozer] *once brought back several Chrysolina menthastri* [a rare leaf beetle that feeds on wild mint] *from a trip to Hampshire. . These he released into his garden where they became well established on his garden mint and thrived for many years. For several years after, his advice as the local beetle expert was sought by anxious neighbours in dealing with a strange new pest that was eating their mint. Don never let on how they got there.*" Lott (1994)

In a recent article on beetle collectors, Marren (2008) classifies them into a small number of "*systematists, who saw beyond the museum drawers to glimpse a much bigger truth*", and larger numbers of "*virtuosos*" who get wrapped up in "*the tough but intellectually unchallenging work of collecting, recording and describing*" and "*misers*", who "*hoard vast collections of specimens without contributing much, if anything, to knowledge or discourse*". According to his rather elitist perspective, the Leicestershire collectors might appear to be representative of the "*misers*", but, in fact, their work has helped to lay the foundations of the modern nature conservation movement. A manuscript list of beetles from the Leighfield Forest was compiled by Clark to provide information for the establishment of one of the first Sites of Special Scientific Interest (SSSI) in Leicestershire. SSSIs now represent the schedule of sites that are legally protected for nature conservation in the UK. The Red Data Book List of British Insects (Shirt 1987) is a list of threatened species that formed the basis for insect species conservation in Britain. It is almost entirely based on the work of similar amateur collectors across Britain. Very few of the records on which it is based were derived from the work of academic or professional biologists active before 1960. The contributions of professional entomologists to the study of Leicestershire beetles at this time were sparse compared to those of the amateur collectors.

A. Roebuck was an entomologist in the agricultural college at Sutton Bonington, but also pursued his entomological interests in his spare time. He was a member of the Biology section of the LLPS and published a series of notes on local Heteroptera before publishing a couple of interesting notes on a rare click beetle and beetles in Kegworth church (Roebuck 1938, Roebuck & Broadbent 1945) C.A. Collingwood, an entomologist working for the Ministry of Agriculture at Shardlow published records of beetles associated with ant nests (Collingwood 1957). Tozer told me that he did not know an A.R. Tindall, who published some beetle records from South Wigston in the south of the city (Tindall 1943). Tindall (1959) also published a note on a caddis-fly and a chironomid, hardly the fare of amateur collectors, and he may have had some professional involvement in entomology. The University College of Leicester was founded in 1921, but its most active zoologist, Professor H.P. Moon, was primarily interested in a variety of freshwater groups and I know of no beetle records emanating from that institution during this period.

It is of great benefit to our knowledge of wildlife in Leicestershire that many of the twentieth century collections have been secured by the museum, but the current physical condition of each collection varies according to the history of each collector's continuing interest in beetles later in life. Taylor and Tozer retained an active interest until shortly before their deaths. Their collections were maintained in good order until their respective transfers to the museum. Henderson seems to have stopped collecting regularly in the 1950s. Although he was persuaded to do some collecting in the sixties and early seventies by the activities of the Loughborough Naturalists' Club, his time was increasingly spent in other interests and caring for his sick wife. His collection suffered significant pest damage before it passed to the museum on his death in 1983. Clark's collecting activities dropped off in the 1940s as a result of a rise in family and professional commitments. A large proportion of his collection was eaten by museum pests, but what remains is nevertheless of great interest and value. Together these collections contain tens of thousands of specimens of Leicestershire and Rutland beetles that give us a picture of which species were living in the two counties during this period.

The collections of Taylor, Henderson, Tozer and Clark are better labelled than those of their Victorian predecessors and they also have a wider geographical scope within Leicestershire and neighbouring counties. Taylor's work took him to churches in different parts of the Leicestershire countryside and he took the opportunity to collect in places previously unvisited by coleopterists. Tozer was severely lame after contracting polio in childhood and had to wear a built-up shoe. He used to go out collecting on his bicycle or moped, but could not easily walk very far from the road. He was adept at finding rare species on roadside verges and hedges. Among his favourite collecting grounds were the limestone areas of Rutland and Northamptonshire, especially the Wansford area. Henderson moved to Loughborough and his collection contains material from several sites in that area of the county, such as Swithland Reservoir and Loughborough Meadows. Because of their sustained interest over a long period of time, the twentieth century collectors acquired more skills for finding rare and cryptic species than Bouskell and his Leicestershire contemporaries, although they still tended to avoid what they regarded as difficult groups, such as the rove beetle family (Staphylinidae). In part this was due to a lack of equipment. In the introduction to his list of beetles from Buddon Wood, Henderson (1975) wrote that:

*"The species list would have been considerably larger had I in my early days been a keen student of that formidable family, the Staphylinidae. For specific determination this family require a binocular microscope and the cost of such was then quite beyond my means."*

Compared to Bouskell, the twentieth century collectors were disinclined to write about the fruits of their endeavours and, for the most part, they were certainly less lyrical when they did so. In the entomological journals, their activities are represented by a scattering of tersely written notes on the capture of rare species. Some of Taylor's notes must be the shortest ever to be accepted for publication and are brief enough for one example from the Entomologist's monthly Magazine to be quoted here in its entirety:

*"Sphindus dubius Gyll. (Col., Sphindidae) new to Leicestershire – On June 21st 1943, I took a specimen of Sphindus dubius Gyll. under bark at Copt Oak. – S. O. Taylor, 34 Nelson Street, Leicester, November 9th 1943."*

In 1933 the British Association for the Advancement of Science again visited Leicester, but the section on beetles provided by Taylor for the associated handbook gives only tantalising glimpses of some of the discoveries made since 1907 (Lowe et al. 1933). All this makes Taylor sound quite dull, but face to face he was obviously a different character. He gave numerous talks to the entomology and biology sections of the LLPS and he was described as having a keen sense of humour. He apparently enjoyed playing practical jokes (Ashurst 1979). This side of Taylor's character surfaces just once in his published work. In a rather whimsical note in the Entomologist's monthly Magazine entitled *"Question of gravity"*, he wrote:

*"Dr. K. G. Blair's interesting article on how a fly alights on the ceiling calls to mind an incident I saw some years ago. A small insect was crawling on the ceiling and then it jumped a few inches further along. I captured it and found it to be a flea. How it did the trick has puzzled me ever since."* (Taylor 1942)

It sounds like a tall story, but he got it published. Taylor represents a vital link between the late Victorian coleopterists and their twentieth century successors. He evidently inspired people to take an interest, not only in beetles, but also natural history in a wider sense. His son became a leading local botanist and he has been credited with kindling the interests of another leading Leicestershire botanist, F.A. Sowter (Primavesi & Evans 1988).

On January 17th 1934, the Zoology section of the LLPS resolved to form a committee, to which Taylor was elected, for the purpose of recording the Leicestershire Fauna (Anon. 1934). In 1948 we read that Taylor was part of:

*"a sub-committee* [of the fauna committee] *formed at the commencement of the winter session to formulate a plan for the ultimate production of a fauna of the two counties* [Leicestershire and Rutland]. *A good start has been made and the sections are indebted to the parent society for a small grant to enable them to obtain the necessary record cards, labels etc. It is hoped however that more members will offer their help in the work. The department of Zoology, University College and the Biology Department, City Museum, have offered all possible help."* (Anon. 1948)

By 1948, Taylor was at the end of his active career and was about to spend the rest of his life bedridden. I have seen no trace of any beetle lists or sets of records resulting from the activities of all these committees. Although they occasionally published additions to the county list, I did not gain the impression that any of the twentieth century collectors were interested in methodically recording the distributions of beetle species in Leicestershire and Rutland. I was therefore surprised when I recently discovered a card index compiled by Tozer in the 1960s, which I think must have come into the museum with his collection. Each card lists records extracted from the museum collections for a particular species together with a summary of its distribution in Leicestershire and Rutland. The card index must have taken a long time to compile and will be a valuable source of information on beetle distribution in the early twentieth century, when it is digitised. In the 1960s and early 70s members of the Loughborough Naturalists' Club persuaded Henderson to write down lists of beetles from a series of locations in the Charnwood area. Unfettered by the editorial restrictions applied to published notes in the entomological journals, they are written in an entertaining style in Henderson's trademark copperplate handwriting:

*"It was with anticipations of considerable interest that I recently received an extract, taken from a turn of the century quarterly issue of the Transactions of the Leicester literary and Philosophical Society.* [The Coleoptera of Bradgate Park by Frederick Bates] *If beetles are not your particular cup of tea, this paper would have seemed to you a rather soulless list of many hundreds of Latin names, almost devoid of any qualifying and interesting annotations and with no indication whether or not the records rested on the capture of a single specimen. Despite this, my anticipations were fully justified. I learned with astonishment and delight of species in the park, whose occurrence there I had not the slightest inkling. Just though to uphold our own modern end of the stick, I would venture to guess that the author would have experienced equal astonishment, could he have known about findings since his time."* Henderson (1962).

*"I cite an instance of the persistence of a species to a locality. Given in Fowler* [Henderson's beetle bible] *was a record for Buddon by W.G. Blatch for the minute staphylinid beetle Atheta subglabra, 2?mm long. Apart from the Buddon record it was only known from Scottish localities. I had a friend staying with me who was a specialist in staphs and was aware of the mentioned record. We had a morning in Buddon and were about to leave the wood when we noticed the base of tree trunk beset by numerous flies. I must admit that I would have passed it over, but my friend immediately remarked 'Ah, just what I wanted – latrine of a fox!.' Running about with the flies were some tiny black staphs. These tiny black beetles were too difficult to accomplish specific identification in the field, but a few days after his return home I received a note from him to the effect that our capture was the rare Atheta subglabra – and the best of British luck."* Henderson (1975).

Together with the evidence provided by the collections that made it safely to the museum, these manuscripts provide us with a valuable record of beetles in Leicestershire in the first half of the twentieth century.

# Coleopterists active in Leicestershire 1908 to 1959

| Name | Born | Died | Active in Leics | Main biographic sources |
|---|---|---|---|---|
| William H Barrow | c1857 | after 8.1945 | 1902-1945 | Reports of section F published in LLPS Transactions, Lott (1984) |
| J.K. Bates | 10.1.1931 | 29.11.1957 | 1945-1952 | Diaries in Museum history files |
| Kenneth John Benjamin Clark | 4.1908 | 4.2001 | 1929-1950 | Collection index, Tozer Catalogue |
| C.A. Collingwood | ? | ? | 1954-1960 | |
| Claude W Henderson | c 1907 | 8.2.1983 | 1922-1972 | Henderson manuscripts |
| A. Roebuck | ? | ? | 1938-1944 | LLPS section reports |
| Trevor William Tailby | 9.3.1915 | 9.2.1968 | 1951-1967 | Collection notebook, Primavesi & Evans (1988) |
| Stephen Oliver Taylor | 1870 | 9.1953 | 1903-1948 | LLPS section reports, Collection notebook, Ashurst (1979) |
| A.R. Tindall | ? | ? | 1942-1943 | Tindall (1943) |
| Donald Tozer | 12.4.1907 | 10.1993 | 1921-1991 | Lott (1994), Evans (1983), Tozer Catalogue |
| W. Turner | ? | ? | 1956-1959 | |
| R. Woodward | ? | ? | 1926-1946 | Tozer catalogue, J.K. Bates diaries |

# Manuscript sources for the period 1908 to 1959

(including sources relating to visiting coleopterists not mentioned in the main text)

W.A.F. Balfour Browne's card index (National Museum of Scotland)

W.A.F. Balfour Browne's Journal (National Museum of Scotland)

C.E. Tottenham's "Collecting Localities" (Natural History Museum, London)

K.J.B. Clark (1955): Record of Coleoptera in the district of Loddington Reddish, Skeffington Wood and Owston Wood (Leicestershire Museums Service)

C. W. Henderson (1975): The Beetles of Buddon Wood (Leicestershire Museums Service)

C. W. Henderson's list of beetles from Swithland Reservoir (Leicestershire Museums Service)

C. W. Henderson: Beetles recorded for the 'Big Meadow' Loughborough circa 1946-47 (Leicestershire Museums Service)

C. W. Henderson: Good beetles for Swithland Wood (Leicestershire Museums Service)

C. W. Henderson (1971): A few interesting notes on Coleoptera for Leicestershire (Leicestershire Museums Service)

C. W. Henderson: A few beetles for Swithland Reservoir (Leicestershire Museums Service)

C. W. Henderson: Cropston Reservoir (Leicestershire Museums Service)

C. W. Henderson (1972): Possible additions to the coleopterous fauna of Bradgate Park, taken during four Saturday mornings in 1972 (Leicestershire Museums Service)

C.A. Collingwood (1960): List of insects captured in Leicestershire and Rutland 1954 – 1960.(Leicestershire Museums Service)

# Main literature sources for Leicestershire beetle records 1908 to 1959

ANON. (1926). Report of section E - Biology. *Transactions of the Leicester Literary and Philosophical Society* **27**: 59.

ANON. (1938). Report of section D, Botany, and section E - Zoology. *Transactions of the Leicester Literary and Philosophical Society* **39**: 42-43.

BARROW, W.H. (1905). A Retrospect of a Season's Collecting Coleoptera, 1904. *Transactions of the Leicester Literary and Philosophical Society* **9**: 81-82.

BARROW, W.H. (1912). Capture of *Aleochara brunneipennis* near Leicester. *Entomologist's Record* **24**: 246.

COLLINGWOOD, C.A. (1957). Myrmecophilous beetles in the Midlands. *Entomologist's Record* **69**: 10-14.

COOTER, J. (1980). A note on *Ernoporus caucasicus* Lind. (Col., Scolytidae) in Britain. *Entomologist's monthly Magazine* **116**: 112.

DIXON, G.B. (1905). Quarterly Reports of the Sections: Section F for Entomology. *Transactions of the Leicester Literary and Philosophical Society* **9**: 81-90.

DONISTHORPE, H.StJ.K. (1941). Coleoptera in Leicestershire. *Entomologist's Record* **53**: 132-133.

DUFFY, E.A.J. (1947). A contribution towards the Biology of *Aromia moschata* L. the "Musk" Beetle. Proceedings of the South London entomological and Natural History Society. **1947-1948**: 82-110.

FOWLER, W.W. & DONISTHORPE, H.StJ.K. (1913). *The Coleoptera of the British Islands*. (Volume 6) London: L. Reeve & Co.

HENDERSON, C.W. (1944). *Bagous lutosus* Gy. and Cryptocephalus frontalis, Marsh in Leicestershire. *Entomologist's monthly Magazine* **80**: 24.

HENDERSON, C.W. (1962). An introduction to the beetles of Bradgate Park and Reservoir. In ANON. *Bradgate Park and Cropston Reservoir margins* Loughborough: Loughborough Naturalists' Club.

KAUFMANN, R.R.U. (1944). British Longicorn records. *Entomologist's monthly Magazine* **80**: 260-261.

KAUFMANN, R.R.U. (1946). British Longicorn records. *Entomologist's monthly Magazine* **82**: 103-104.

KAUFMANN, R.R.U. (1947). British Longicorn records. *Entomologist's monthly Magazine* **83**: 84-87.

LAST, H.R. (1955). Two new British species of Staphylinidae. *Entomologist's monthly Magazine* **91**: 106.

LOWE, E.E., MAYES, W.E., WAGSTAFFE, R. & TAYLOR, S.O. (1933). The Zoology of Leicestershire. In: BRYAN, P.W. (ed.) *A Scientific Study of Leicester and District*. London: British Association for the Advancement of Science.

PEARCE, E.J. (1945). All the British Haliplidae taken during 1939. *Entomologist's monthly Magazine* **81**: 80.

PEARCE, E.J. (1948). Pselaphidae - new county records. *Entomologist's monthly Magazine* **84**: 87-89.

ROEBUCK, A. (1938). Beetles in a church. *Entomologist's monthly Magazine* **74**: 209.

ROEBUCK, A. & BROADBENT, L. (1945). Some notes on *Cryptohypnus quadripustulatus* F. on grass fields in the Midlands. *Entomologist's monthly Magazine* **81**: 8.

TAYLOR, S.O. (1943). Two beetles new to Leicestershire. *Entomologist's monthly Magazine* **79**: 183.

TAYLOR, S.O. (1943). *Sphindus dubius*, Gyll. new to Leicestershire. *Entomologist's monthly Magazine* **79**: 277.

TINDALL, A.R. (1943). Records of Coleoptera at South Wigston, Leicester. *Entomologist's monthly Magazine* **79**: 113.

TOZER, D. (1941). *Anthicus bifasciatus* Roni. (Col. Anthicidae) in the Midland counties. *Entomologist's monthly Magazine* **77**: 278.

TOZER, D. (1942). *Anthicus tobias* Mars.in Huntingdonshire and Leicestershire. *Entomologist's monthly Magazine* **78**: 14.

TOZER, D. (1943). Notes on the occurrence of *Platyrhinus resinosus*. Scop. in the Midlands. *Entomologist's monthly Magazine* **79**: 62-63.

TOZER, D. (1944). Notes on Midland Coleoptera for 1943. *Entomologist's monthly Magazine* **80**: 21.

TOZER, D. (1947). Notes on Coleoptera collecting for 1946. *Entomologist's monthly Magazine* **84**: 47.

TOZER, D. (1947). *Plagiodera versicolora* Laich. (Col. Chrysomelidae) in Leicestershire. *Entomologist's monthly Magazine* **84**: 55.

WALLIS, H.H. (1919). On the aquatic Coleoptera of the Trent valley in the neighbourhood of Long Eaton. *Entomologist's monthly Magazine* **55**: 127-128.

WHITTINGHAM, W.G. (1909). Reports of the Sections: Section F Entomology. *Transactions of the Leicester Literary and Philosophical Society* **13**: 152-154.

# 1960 – 1981  The age of recorders

The natural history scene in Leicestershire was rejuvenated at the beginning of the sixties by a series of events. The first was the arrival at Leicester Museum in July 1959 of Ian Evans, an energetic and infectiously enthusiastic recorder of the natural environment. At the same time, groups of naturalists around the county banded together to form local natural history societies in order to share their interests and record the flora and fauna of their local patch.

Prominent among these was the Loughborough Naturalists' Club founded in 1960. John Crocker, a founder member, told me that the idea for the club was conceived by a group of local naturalists sheltering under a railway bridge during a rain-storm. Right from the start, the activities of the club focussed on recording wildlife and publishing the records in its newsletter, *Heritage*. A target area for recording was defined covering Charnwood Forest and adjacent areas of the Soar valley. Survey units within this area were allocated to individual members. Several reports on individual survey units were published and the work as a whole culminated in the publication of a book dealing with landscape history and the results of contemporary land use survey (Crocker 1981). Individual members also took on responsibility for co-ordinating the recording of particular groups of plants and animals. Several invertebrate groups were well covered. John Crocker covered the spiders and eventually published the first comprehensive account of spiders in Leicestershire and Rutland (Crocker & Daws 1996, 2001). Peter Gamble and Jack Ward invested in a portable generator and enthusiastically light-trapped the area for moths over a long period. Initially, it was conceived that Claude Henderson would cover the beetles. He was persuaded to come out of retirement to write a valuable chapter on beetles for the report on Bradgate Park (Henderson 1962) and make occasional recording forays, but by the sixties, Henderson's interests had moved on and his heart was not really in it. Instead, Harry Clements, who worked for the Ministry of Agriculture became interested in both beetles and plant bugs (Heteroptera). With the encouragement of Ian Evans, Clements produced a manuscript list of ground beetles (Carabidae). This was never published, although a similar list of plant bugs was (Clements & Evans 1973) and this contains useful details of Clements' collecting sites. Clements' initial burst of enthusiasm in the mid sixties was not sustained and in 1984 he donated his collection to the museum. John Crocker, Peter Gamble and Anthony Squires were other club members, who collected beetles and passed them to Henderson or Clements for identification, but it is fair to say that they had a casual interest in beetles and concentrated their activities on other areas of natural history.

The Rutland Natural History Society was also very active in recording. As in the Loughborough Naturalists' Club, individual members took responsibility for co-ordinating the recording of particular groups of plants and animals. Records of ladybirds and other easily identified beetles frequently appear in their newsletter and publications. Linda Worrall later co-ordinated a series of glow-worm surveys that monitored populations of this declining species. However, no members emerged with a special interest in beetles as a whole and the majority of beetle species remained unrecorded.

Across the two counties as a whole, wildlife recording was stimulated and supported from the museum. Soon after his arrival, Evans' energy and organisational abilities ensured his swift promotion to a level of responsibility within the museum hierarchy. From this position he built up the staff and resources needed to develop one of the first local record centres in the country. Evans had a strongly articulated  vision of  naturalists  meticulously  recording the wildlife of Leicestershire and Rutland.

The geographical unit for recording was defined as the Watsonian vice-county number 55 (Leicestershire and Rutland), a unit that had been widely used by both botanists and zoologists since its inception in the nineteenth century. He set up a labyrinthine series of paper record files that still underpin the record centre operations in the current digital age. Records of species were placed in a series of systematic files divided up taxonomically. Site records containing both habitat and species data were allocated to a series of files allocated to civil parishes and containing sub-folders for special sites. Biographical details were added to a series of personality files, which provided much of the information used to write this book. A separate series of "history files" covered material accessioned into the museum collections and contained field notebooks and collection registers compiled by the original collectors. Evans considered himself to have a special interest in several groups of wildlife. In fact, there were not many taxa that were excluded from these areas of interest. He set up personal research files for each of these projects. All files contained numerous cross-referencing slips linked to original source documents in other file series through long and complex filing codes. Evans was totally acquisitive of detailed records, complete with Ordnance Survey grid references, to populate this vast system of files and of specimens to add to the museum collections for reference and to act as voucher specimens for paper records.

As well as putting in place structures for building a comprehensive body of wildlife records, Evans also inspired people to go out and generate the records. He appointed Jan Dawson, John Mathias and Anthony Fletcher to carry out curatorial duties on the museum collections and they were also expected to take a lead in recording particular aspects of the counties' wildlife. Their duties were prescribed in some detail and it is fair to say that in modern parlance, he engaged in "micro-management" methods that included going through the wastepaper bins of some staff members. He rigorously checked the written work of his staff, which would be returned liberally annotated with grammatical and stylistic corrections. When the second draft was resubmitted for approval, it was not unusual for sentences to be corrected back to the original wording. The museum also took on trainee natural history assistants on three year contracts, who followed a post-graduate certificate studies course at the University of Leicester Department of Museum Studies. One of these was Howard Mendel, who developed his interest in beetles while at Leicester and went on to become a leading British coleopterist firstly at Ipswich Museum and then the Natural History Museum (London). Several technicians were employed to carry out taxidermy and other specimen preparations and they were also encouraged to go out and record wildlife. Derek Foxwell and R.D. Osborne collected several beetles that are now in the museum collections. A few small collections of insects were received at this time from donors around the county, often operating in areas that had been previously neglected for beetles, but this material mainly represented easily collected species and none of these individuals went on to develop a special expertise in beetles.

Early in the sixties, Evans started a Saturday club at the museum for children interested in natural history. Its members included Don Goddard, who quickly developed a passion for insects and in particular beetles and bugs. Several of the consequent records that he sent into the museum at this time were generated while he was still fourteen years old. The sixties was an era of youth rebellion and Goddard with his long hair and wild-eyed look fitted the hippy image very well. He famously used to turn up wearing open-toed sandals to play snooker at the Conservative Club, where his father was a prominent member (Alexander & Lott 2001). Inspired by his interest in insects, Goddard studied Biological Sciences at the University of Leicester before joining the British Antarctic Survey as an invertebrate ecologist researching Antarctic soil mites from 1971 to 1977.

He spent two years based in South Georgia, where he endured temperatures of -40ºC and had to resort to collecting frozen mosses with a felling axe and drill. In 1978, Evans instituted a detailed and comprehensive survey of the flora and fauna of three areas in north-east Leicestershire in order to gather information for a response to a proposal to exploit coal reserves. He contracted Goddard to survey the beetles and other insects. This work was followed by further contracts to survey insects at sites scattered all over Leicestershire and Rutland. These surveys established the interest of several sites of importance for insect conservation for the first time. In 1983, now married and with responsibilities, Goddard left Leicestershire for a teaching position in Worcestershire.

The explosion in wildlife recording that took place in the sixties and seventies resulted in the publication of county lists of dragonflies, stoneflies, caddis-flies, plant bugs and water bugs, while extensive records of butterflies and moths were regularly published in various newsletters. In this context, the results for beetles have to be seen as relatively disappointing. It is difficult to know why this is. The standard reference work for beetles (Joy 1932) was now out-of date and perhaps did not compare favourably with the more attractive illustrated guides that had started to appear for other groups. Marren (2008) attributed the popularity of beetles in Victorian times to their suitability for forming a collection. They look good when preserved in collections and present a challenge to find. Perhaps the shift in emphasis from collecting to recording may have reduced their comparative allure. I do not really accept all these arguments. Beetles are just as much fun to record as they are to collect. In addition, the volume of contemporary published notes in the popular entomological press suggests no sign of diminution of interest in other parts of the country. The most likely reasons for the poor showing of beetles in the initial Leicestershire recording boom are the vicissitudes of fortune.

It is undoubtedly the case that we are still in the age of recorders. Since 1981 wildlife recording in the two counties has continued unabated. The Leicestershire Entomological Society was formed in 1988 and beetles have attracted more attention. There are now 60,000 beetle records held in the electronic database of the local record centre. I became interested in freshwater invertebrates around 1980 after attending an evening class given by Max Wade at Loughborough University. I had already joined the Loughborough Naturalists' Club, where I met Peter Gamble, probably the most knowledgeable general naturalist in the county at that time. He introduced me to many local sites of interest and I expanded my activities to cover a wide range of insect groups. At the end of 1981, Ian Evans invited me into the museum and suggested to me that I ought to concentrate my effort on one group in order to make an impact on our knowledge of Leicestershire insects. I asked him which group he recommended and he replied, "*Beetles*". On 3rd January 1982 I collected 26 beetle species from flood refuse by the River Soar and I am still on beetles over twenty five years later. In 1983 I applied for the position of graduate trainee at Leicestershire Museums Service and was agreeably surprised to be offered the job. I quit my well paid teaching post for more meagre remuneration and soon discovered that I had entered paradise. Every morning at eight I would be outside the front doors of the museum waiting for them to be opened, so that I could start work. In my work I discovered the exploits of former generations of coleopterists whose two hundred years of endeavour encompassed ground-breaking scientific theories and the narrowest of special interests, epic voyages to exotic parts of the globe and isolated lives spent in country parishes, good luck and bad luck, fame and obscurity, but most of all an enduring fascination with an endless well of natural curiosity.

And the best of British luck!

# Coleopterists active in Leicestershire 1960 to 1981

| Name | Born | Died | Active in Leics | Main biographic sources |
|------|------|------|-----------------|-------------------------|
| Harry A.B. Clements | | | 1962-1973 | |
| Donald George Goddard | 14.8.1947 | 6.2000 | 1961-1983 | Alexander & Lott (2001) |
| Howard Mendel | | | 1975-1977 | |

# Manuscript sources for the period 1960 to 1981

H.A.B. Clements' list of Leicestershire Carabidae (Leicestershire Museums Service)

# Primary literature sources for Leicestershire beetle records 1960 to 1981

DAVIES, B.N.K. (1980). Clipsham Quarries: Their history and evolution. *Transactions of the Leicester Literary and Philosophical Society* **72**: 59-68.

EVANS, M.S. (1979). *Leistus rufomarginatus* (Duft.) (Col., Carabidae) in Leicestershire. *Entomologist's monthly Magazine* **114**: 125.

GODDARD, D.G. (1979). Beetles. In Evans, I.M. (ed.) *North-east Leicestershire Coalfield. Report of a biological survey, 1978* pp 157-196, Leicester: Leicestershire Museums, Art Galleries and Records Service.

GODDARD, D.G. (1985). *Anobium inexpectatum* Lohse (Col., Anobiidae) in Leicestershire. *Entomologist's monthly Magazine* **121**: 157.

GODDARD, D.G. (1986). *Dytiscus circumcinctus* Ahrens (Col., Dytiscidae) in Leicestershire. *Entomologist's monthly Magazine* **122**: 7.

LEECH, M.J. (1965). *Hylecoetus dermestoides* L. (Col., Lymexylonidae) in Leicestershire. *Entomologist's record* **77**: 235.

MATHIAS, J.H. (1979). Fauna - freshwater invertebrates. In Evans, I.M. (ed.) *North-east Leicestershire Coalfield. Report of a biological survey, 1978* pp 87-120, Leicester: Leicestershire Museums, Art Galleries and Records Service.

SKIDMORE, P. (1962). *Insects in 1960 (Part one). Entomologist's record* **74**: 155-161.

# Changes in the Leicestershire beetle fauna

The Leicestershire coleopterists have witnessed many changes over 200 years, as some species declined in numbers or disappeared completely, while other new species arrive on the scene. These changes can be observed at the county scale and perhaps even more so at two individual sites that have been studied over a long period: Bradgate Park and Buddon Wood.

## Bradgate Park

*"We Leicestershire people are all proud of our Bradgate Park: and well does it deserve its high reputation and our affectionate regard. It has just claims to be considered the most attractive and picturesque locality in our county, if not in our country. Its manifold natural beauties; its bold and rugged elevations commanding most magnificent prospects; its babbling brook and waterfalls; its craggy dells; its grand old oaks; its picturesque ruins and famous historical associations; all combine to make it a spot to be at once beloved and venerated."* (Bates 1896)

Bradgate Park now receives over a million visitors a year, but it was first set up in mediaeval times as a deer park, which provided both sport and wood for fuel (Stevenson & Squires 1994). The trees would have been specially managed by pollarding, a technique involving cutting branches and successive shoots at a height of eight to ten feet. This made for hard work, but it provided both a regular crop of poles and protection from browsing deer. It also prolonged the lives of the trees and it is this practice, which is responsible for the presence of the magnificent ancient oaks at Bradgate today. The acidic Pre-cambrian rocks of Bradgate sustain a covering of heath-grassland on sandy soils over the hills and once gave rise to flushes with patches of *Sphagnum* moss between the hills. Most of these flushes are now drained, but one small remnant still survives near Old John. Three main streams run off Charnwood Forest and where they leave the plateau they form small ravines, in which fast-flowing water once cascaded over moss-covered boulders. One of these ravines is in the park on the River Lin near what is now the main Newtown Linford entrance, presumably Bates' *craggy dell*. The stream there was modified in the late nineteenth century by building pools to intercept silt upstream of the newly constructed Cropston Reservoir. Below the ravine, the stream slows and meanders as a *babbling brook* depositing small shingle beds and cutting earth cliffs into the banks, all valuable habitats for insects.

Bradgate became a focus of entomological activity when Henry Bates cut his teeth on beetles there in the 1840s and it became the favoured destination for his gypsy parties composed of fellow entomologists and lady-friends. His brother, Frederick, continued collecting there after Henry left for the Amazon and in 1855 it received a visit from the celebrated coleopterist, J.A. Power. In the 1890s Bradgate once again became a centre of attention and attracted frequent excursions from the entomology section of the Leicester Literary and Philosophical Society. In 1895, Frederick Bates, C.B. Headly and J.H. Woolley worked the park diligently before Bates published his list of 507 beetle species from Bradgate (Bates 1896). It is not possible from this list to tell what was recorded in the 1890s and what was recorded in the earlier period of activity in the 1840s and 50s, but more detail is available for some species from manuscripts and earlier publications (e.g. Bates 1849). Local collectors continued to visit the park until the 1960s and Henderson (1962) discussed the additions made after 1895. Since then, access to the park for studying beetles has not always been straightforward, except for making casual observations. I was able to look at wetland beetles between 1982 and 1985 and in 1989 and 1990 Ian Evans secured permission for me to sample a wider variety of habitats including the ancient oaks.

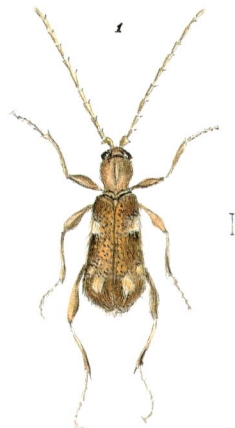

1

Ptinus sexpunctatus, Pz.
In the nests of sparrows.
Common at Long Whatton.

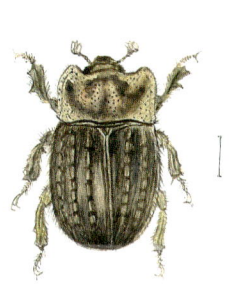

2

Trox scaber, L.
In the nests of owls
Woodpeckers & Sand Martins
Bradgate Park & Quorn.

3

Onthophilus sulcatus, F.
In the nests of Moles

4

Dendrophilus punctatus, Hbst.
In the nests of Owls & in the nest
of the ant Formica rufa. Quorn.

5

Choleva spadicea, Stm.
In the nest of the Mole.
Charnwood district

6

Nemadus colonoides, Kr.
In the nest of Woodpeckers
Quorn Wood.

Drawings of beetles made by Claude Henderson

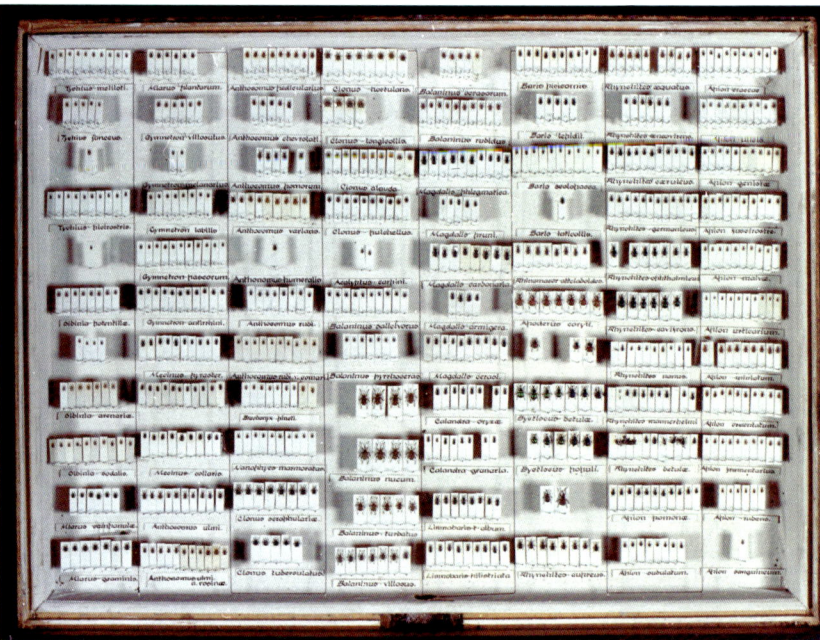

An original drawer from the collection of Claude Henderson complete with handwritten labels

The Musk Beetle was well known at Barrow upon Soar where it used to breed in osiers

Ancient oaks at Bradgate Park provide habitats for many rare beetles

*Calosoma inquisitor,* a former
Buddon Wood speciality. It
climbs oak trees at night to
feed on caterpillars

The Green Tiger Beetle has
been seen regularly at
Bradgate Park since the 1840s

Some of Bradgate's more colourful beetles live in the dry, sandy heath-grassland areas. The Green Tiger Beetle, *Cicindela campestris*, has larvae that construct vertical tunnels in bare sandy soil, from which they catch passing ants. This species was first noted by James Harley in his diary for 1842 and was also a favourite of the brothers Bates. At that time it also occurred in the sandy fields along Anstey Lane leading to the park. It still occurs at Bradgate Park. The sandy tracks at Hallgates are the best places to see them and a sunny day in June is the best time. Watch out for a green beetle that flies along the track for several yards as you approach it. The metallic-coloured click beetle, *Selatosomus aeneus*, is another heath grassland species that has been recorded at Bradgate Park since the 1840s. It is normally found hiding under stones. Several of the more noticeable grassland species that can still be found are dung beetles. The Minotaur Beetle, *Typhaeus typhoeus*, whose males are armed with horns and *Geotrupes vernalis*, one of several violet-coloured dor-beetles are both Bradgate specialities together with two smaller species associated with deer dung, *Aphodius zenkeri* and *A. borealis*.

## Heath-grassland beetles recorded at Bradgate Park in 1848

(Species common in other habitats and species with uncertain identities are not listed)

| Species | Subsequent records |
| --- | --- |
| *Notiophilus aquaticus*, a ground beetle | recorded occasionally up to 1966 |
| *Amara tibialis*, a ground beetler | recorded occasionally up to 1990 |
| *Syntomus foveatus*, a ground beetle | recorded occasionally up to 2003 |
| *Geotrupes stercorosus*, a dor beetle | recorded occasionally up to 1992 |
| *Geotrupes vernalis*, a dor beetle | recorded occasionally up to 1992 |
| *Typhaeus typhoeus*, Minotaur Beetle | recorded frequently up to 1984 |
| *Serica brunnea*, a chafer | recorded occasionally up to 1989 |
| *Byrrhus fasciatus,* a pill beetle | recorded occasionally up to 1938 |
| *Prosternon tessellatus*, a click beetle | none; modern records from elsewhere in Charnwood |
| *Ctenicera cuprea*, a click beetle | recorded frequently up to 1983 |
| *Selatosomus aeneus*, a click beetle | recorded frequently up to 1977 |
| *Orthocerus clavicornis* | not recorded since from anywhere in Leics or Rutland |
| *Timarcha goettingensis*, a leaf beetle | not recorded since 1860s/70s (Holyoak) |
| *Galeruca tanaceti*, a leaf beetle | not recorded since 1850; also from Swithland in 1928 |
| *Apion haematodes*, a weevil | recorded occasionally up to 1952 |
| *Otiorhynchus ovatus*, a weevil | none; modern record from Beacon Hill |
| *Caenopsis fissirostris*, a weevil | recorded occasionally up to 1942 |
| *Trachyphloeus aristatus*, a weevil | none; modern records from East Leics |
| *Trachyphloeus bifoveolatus*, a weevil | recorded occasionally up to 1943 |
| *Neliocarus faber*, a weevil | recorded occasionally up to 1945 |
| *Neliocarus nebulosus,* a weevil | none; modern records from Buddon Wood |
| *Brachysomus echinatus*, a weevil | none since 1854; modern records from East Leics |
| *Micrelus ericae*, a weevil | none; modern records from High Sharpley |
| *Rhinoncus castor*, a weevil | recorded occasionally up to 1949 |

Throughout 1848 Frederick Bates concentrated his efforts on the southern aspects of "*several bold rocky ridges, whose rugged slopes are slightly covered with a loose, gritty, sandy soil, supporting light mossy-grassy vegetation, and covered here and there with chippings of the slate rocks that generally crop out at their summits.*" He listed 41 species from this habitat (Bates 1849), several of which have not been seen since (see table above). I did not work this habitat when I was on the park in the 1980s, so the absence of recent records does not necessarily mean that these species are extinct. *Chrysomela populi* is an impressive orange and green leaf beetle that feeds on dwarf willow and was recorded in 1848 in damp places in the hills. It has not been seen since. Drainage has all but removed the habitat for this species and also species associated with Sphagnum moss, although there is little evidence from the 1896 list of a very diverse Sphagnum fauna to begin with (see table below).

## *Sphagnum* flush and damp heath beetles represented in the 1896 Bradgate Park list

| Species | Subsequent records |
| --- | --- |
| *Hydroporus gyllenhalii*, a diving beetle | recorded again in 1985 |
| *Hydroporus longulus*, a diving beetle | recorded again in 1985 |
| *Enochrus ochropterus*, a water beetle | not recorded since 1896 |
| *Ochthephilum fracticorne*, a rove beetle | recorded again in 1939 |
| *Chrysomela populi*, a leaf beetle | not recorded since 1848 (Henderson 1962) |

The beetles of the River Lin have enjoyed mixed fortunes (see table below). Several interesting species still occur, but they are difficult to see for the casual observer. *Ptenidium brenskei* is less than a millimetre long and lives in the gaps between the gravel at the side of the stream. It is not known from anywhere else in Leicestershire and possibly the Midlands. The Hairy Whirlygig Beetle, *Orectochilus villosus*, hides by day under stones on the bank, but comes out at night to skim over the water surface hunting for insects trapped in the surface tension. *Dianous coerulescens* is a dark metallic blue rove beetle with red spots on its wing case. It too can skate over the water surface, but probably does this to escape from danger as much as any other reason. It spends most of its time hiding in damp moss growing on the weirs between the pools near Newtown Linford. It is often found on waterfalls and is probably a survivor from the time before the silt traps were constructed when the River Lin flowed over moss-covered boulders.

## Some of the rarer beetles of the River Lin

| Species | Recorded dates |
| --- | --- |
| *Bembidion tibiale*, a ground beetle | 1855 to 1897 but none since |
| *Orectochilus villosus*, Hairy Whirlygig | 1895 to 1985 |
| *Hydraena minutissima*, a water beetle | not recorded since 1855 (Power) |
| *Ochthebius exsculptus*, a water beetle | 1855 to 1990 |
| *Ptenidium brenskei* | only discovered in 1990 |
| *Dianous coerulescens*, a rove beetle | 1895 to 1983 |
| *Donacia bicolora*, a reed beetle | not recorded since 1845 (Kirby) |

The ancient oaks provide homes for a large number of the rarer Bradgate species. Many of these make their living out of wood decay, either feeding directly on dead tissue or the fungi that are breaking it down, or on other insects that live in the same place. A really ancient tree is like a beetle metropolis with different species exploiting different parts of the tree. Some species can be found only in rotting heartwood. Others live in bird nests in damp hollows created by wood decay. Some like it hot in sun-drenched dead branches up in the crown. There are specialised species with flattened bodies for living under bark, while other specialists breed only in the bracket fungi growing out of the dead wood.

## Some of the rarer beetles of the ancient oaks

| Species | Microhabitat | Recorded dates |
|---|---|---|
| Ampedus balteatus | Heartrot | 1844 to 1990 |
| Dexiogyia corticina | Under bark | 1860 to 1895 |
| Hedobia imperialis | Dead branches | from before 1896 to 1942 |
| Thymalus limbatus | Under bark | from before 1896 to 1942 |
| Ennearthron cornutum | Bracket fungi | 1895 |
| Conopalpus testaceus | Dead branches | 1895 to 1989 |
| Malthinus frontalis | Dead branches | 1895 to 1989 |
| Phloiotrya vaudoueri | Bracket fungi | 1896 to 1983 |
| Anthocomus fasciatus | Dry heartwood? | 1906 |
| Acrulia inflata | Under bark | 1933 to 1989 |
| Euglenes oculatus | Heartrot | 1937 to 1989 |
| Aplocnemus impressus | Dead branches | 1938 to 1947 |
| Phymatodes testaceus | Under bark | 1941 to 1944 |
| Dendroxena quadrimaculata | Foliage | 1947 |
| Tritoma bipustulata | Bracket fungi | 1972 |
| Ctesias serra | Spider webs | 1980 |
| Eledona agricola | Bracket fungi | 1980 to 1984 |
| Mycetophagus piceus | Heartrot | 1983 |
| Bibloporus minutus | Under bark | 1983 to 1990 |
| Triphyllus bicolor | Bracket fungi | 1984 to 1989 |
| Oxypoda recondita | Heartrot | 1984 to 1989 |
| Scaphisoma boleti | Bracket fungi | 1989 |
| Dorcatoma chrysomelina | Heartrot | 1989 |
| Nossidium pilosellum | Heartrot | 1989 |
| Plectophloeus nitidus | Heartrot | 1989 |
| Nemadus colonoides | Tree hollows | 1989 to 1990 |
| Notolaemus unifasciatus | Under bark | 1989 to 1990 |

Henry Bates discovered the first of these wood decay species as early as April 1844, when he examined some rotten oak wood and found *Ampedus balteatus*, a click beetle with striking red and black wing cases. It still occurs at Bradgate. Harry Holyoak added another rotten wood species, the Rhinoceros Beetle, *Sinodendron cylindricum*, in the 1860s or 70s, although this record was overlooked by Bates (1896). In 1896 Frederick Bates listed eight species that live in bracket fungi and twenty four species that live under bark, almost certainly by examining fallen branches. There is little evidence that he looked in other microhabitats. Twenty one further wood-decay species could well have been taken in flight or on flowers. When recording the twentieth century addition of fifteen wood-decay species and further oak tree foliage species to the Bradgate list, Henderson (1962) pointed out that many of them were "*ancient forest*" species and unlikely to have been absent from the park during the nineteenth century. Even quite common species were omitted from the 1896 list. The acorn weevil, *Curculio venosus*, and the longhorn beetle, *Leiopus nebulosus*, can both be taken easily by beating foliage over a tray with a stick. It is curious that, whereas we now regard the beetles of the veteran oaks as a priority for conservation, the nineteenth century coleopterists seem to have paid only passing attention to them. While they were sweep-netting, looking under stones and examining carrion, dung and moss, a host of rare beetles was looking on unmolested from their oak tree fortresses. Since 1896 the list of wood-decay species has nearly doubled and there has been a steady increase in the number of wood-decay species listed from the park over 150 years. Henderson was probably correct in suggesting that many species, especially those associated with stable habitats such as heartrot, have been living in the park all the time. Many of these species are very difficult to find and their discovery depends largely on serendipity. The burst of new species in the 1980s was due in no small part to the development of new techniques and expertise in finding some of the more cryptic species. It is no wonder that many species eluded the notice of previous generations of coleopterists. However, I think it is quite possible that other species associated with ephemeral habitats such as dead branches and bark come and go more frequently. These species develop in microhabitats that last only for a couple of years before becoming unsuitable and they need to fly off to find new breeding sites regularly. They may well be susceptible to local extinctions, before recolonisation from habitats outside the park. Species that have definitely colonised the park since Bates' time include exotic species originating from America or New Zealand such as *Tetropium gabrieli*, *Ptinella errabunda* and *Euophryum confine*.

# Buddon Wood

"*It is clear that Buddon supported woodland in one form or another without a break from at least 1086* [the time of the Domesday Book] *and probably very long before that to the present century…. The prominent nature of the hill together with the beauty of its spring greenness was a delight for nineteenth century travellers along what was to become the A6. The granite core was covered in most places by a very shallow layer of largely acid soil which in places was entirely absent, as the ancient rocks outcropped at the surface. Elsewhere deep accumulations of peat and humus could be found. In spite of the unpromising conditions, individual trees, especially oaks, of the natural woodland sometimes reached a great size.*" (Squires & Jeeves 1994).

Buddon Wood was a special place in the nineteenth century. It has the highest recorded number of ancient woodland plants in Leicestershire and probably amongst the highest recorded in Britain (Squires & Jeeves 1994). It is one of three Leicestershire woodlands to hold substantial populations of the Sessile Oak and it also contains stands of another ancient woodland tree species, the Small-leaved Lime (Jeeves 1996). It was into this enchanted world that Frank Plant stepped to discover the weevil, *Tropideres sepicola*, new to Britain in 1856. He also discovered another rare weevil, *Trachodes hispidus* and Buddon soon became a magnet for coleopterists from across the Midlands. One of Buddon's greatest attractions for these coleopterists was the rich beetle fauna associated with the nests of the wood ant, *Formica rufa*. Donisthorpe studied ant nest beetles here between 1897 and 1909 and they continued to be recorded until the 1950s (Collingwood, 1957).

Henderson's (1975) list of Buddon beetles is a valuable summary of the recorded fauna of the wood while it was still intact and in good condition. The demise of Buddon Wood as one of the best ancient woodlands in Britain began in the Second World War, when the stands of mature Sessile Oaks and other trees were clear-felled and allowed to regenerate naturally (Jeeves 1996). Silver birch took over much of the wood, but many of the oaks and limes were able to produce coppice growth. Then further extensive damage to the woodland was caused by fires in the 1950s. Quarrying of road-stone began in the early 1970s and Buddon now contains one the deepest holes of human origin in Europe. The centre of the wood has been obliterated leaving a rim of woodland. Nevertheless, the remaining areas of sessile oak wood still retain a magical atmosphere that gives a glimpse of what it must once have been like to enter Buddon to look for beetles. In 1995 I was asked to survey this remnant for beetles concentrating on the leaf litter and wood decay fauna (Jeeves 1996).

The most obvious casualties of the changes at Buddon are the ant nest beetles. The Red Wood Ant became extinct at the wood in the 1960s (P.H. Gamble, pers. comm.) and all but two of the beetles that depended on it went with it. The nearest place that you can find them now is about forty miles away in Bedford Purlieus in Northamptonshire. The other two species can occur independently of wood ants in the red-rotten heartwood of old oaks and could conceivably survive unnoticed at Buddon.

## Ant nest beetles recorded at Buddon in the 1870s and 1880s

| Species | Date of last record | Current status in Leicestershire |
| --- | --- | --- |
| *Eutheia plicata*, a scydmaenid beetle | 1880s | extinct |
| *Lyprocorrhe anceps*, a rove beetle | 1897 | extinct |
| *Zyras humeralis*, a rove beetle | 1901 | extinct |
| *Stenichnus godarti*, a scydmaenid beetle | 1905 | no recent records |
| *Monotoma angusticollis* | 1909 | extinct |
| *Ptenidium formicetorum* | 1909 | extinct |
| *Monotoma conicicollis* | 1933 | extinct |
| *Myrmetes piceus*, a histerid beetle | 1933 | extinct |
| *Leptacinus formicetorum*, a rove beetle | 1937 | extinct |
| *Clytra quadripunctata*, a leaf beetle | 1942 | extinct |
| *Dendrophilus pygmaeus*, a histerid beetle | 1950s | extinct |
| *Dinarda maerkeli*, a rove beetle | 1950s | extinct |
| *Gyrohypnus atratus*, a rove beetle | 1950s | extinct |
| *Notothecta flavipes*, a rove beetle | 1950s | extinct |
| *Oxypoda formiceticola*, a rove beetle | 1950s | extinct |
| *Oxypoda recondita*, a rove beetle | 1950s | rare |
| *Quedius brevis*, a rove beetle | 1950s | extinct |
| *Thiasophila angulata*, a rove beetle | 1950s | extinct |

## Some of the rarer canopy foliage species recorded at Buddon

| Species | Food source | Recorded dates |
| --- | --- | --- |
| *Calosoma inquisitor*, a ground beetle | caterpillars | 1855 to 1943 |
| *Chrysomela aenea*, a leaf beetle | alder | 1855 |
| *Crepidodera nitidula*, a flea beetle | aspen | 1880s |
| *Dendroxena quadrimaculata*, a silphid beetle | caterpillars | 1894 to 1937 |
| *Lasiorhynchites cavifrons*, a weevil | oak twigs | 1897 to 1939 |
| *Lasiorhynchites olivaceus*, a weevil | oak twigs | 1856 to 1995 |
| *Podabrus alpinus*, a soldier beetle | predator | up to 1943 |
| *Rhagonycha translucida*, a soldier beetle | predator | 1940s |

Beetles of the canopy foliage have fared scarcely better than the ant nest species. Many of the rarer species have not been seen since the wood was clear felled during the war. One high profile casualty is the ground beetle, *Calosoma inquisitor*, so beloved of Harry Holyoak. Although it is technically a ground beetle, *C. inquisitor*'s distinguishing characteristic is that it climbs trees at night to hunt caterpillars in the canopy. It is therefore a genuine woodland creature. Buddon was its last remaining Leicestershire site, so when it disappeared from Buddon, it disappeared from the county.

# Some of the rarer wood-decay beetles of Buddon Wood

| Species | Microhabitat | Recorded dates |
|---|---|---|
| Calambus bipustulatus | Heartrot | 1853 |
| Trachodes hispidus | Leaf litter | 1854 to 1995 |
| Agrilus laticollis | Dead branches | 1855 to 1995 |
| Tropideres sepicola | Dead branches | 1856 to 1942 |
| Dissoleucas niveirostris | Dead branches | 1860 |
| Ampedus balteatus | Heartrot | 1860s to 1950s |
| Acalles ptinoides | Leaf litter | 1860s to 1995 |
| Acalles roboris | Leaf litter | 1871 to 1995 |
| Acalles misellus | Dead branches | 1890s to 1920s |
| Prionocyphon serricornis | Rot holes | 1890s to 1924 |
| Poecilium alni | Dead branches | 1890s to 1934 |
| Conopalpus testaceus | Dead branches | undated (Henderson) |
| Eledona agricola | Bracket fungi | undated (Henderson) |
| Hedobia imperialis | Dead branches | undated (Henderson) |
| Orchesia micans | Bracket fungi | undated (Henderson) |
| Melandrya caraboides | Heartrot | 1928 |
| Hallomenus binotatus | Bracket fungi | 1940 |
| Cryptarcha strigata | Sap runs | 1941 |
| Abdera quadrifasciata | Dead branches | 1945 to 1995 |
| Enicmus brevicornis | Mouldy bark | 1995 |
| Enicmus testaceus | Slime fungi | 1995 |
| Ernoporus caucasicus | Under bark | 1995 |
| Lissodema cursor | Dead branches | 1995 |
| Melasis buprestoides | Dead branches | 1995 |
| Ptenidium gressneri | Heartrot | 1995 |

The attractively marked weevil, *Tropideres sepicola*, first found by Plant was rediscovered in 1942 by Don Tozer when he was collecting in the parkland area of Buddon with Claude Henderson. Tozer remarked to Henderson that he had heard that *Tropideres* was originally taken by Plant by beating faggots lying on the ground, so he picked up some sticks and shook them over a sheet. One promptly dropped out. I have found *T. sepicola* only on aerial branches (in Worcestershire), but another of Buddon's rare weevils, *Trachodes*, together with two *Acalles* species, occur in leaf litter, where they appear to be associated with fungi growing on fallen twigs and other pieces of dead wood [*]. They can be very difficult to find in the field, because when they drop onto the sheet, they play dead and are indistinguishable from small pieces of litter. Even when they move, they move very slowly. Henderson (1975) describes how he took all three of the then known British species of *Acalles* in the first year that he visited Buddon, but then never saw any of them again. A useful tip that I received from Peter Hodge, a Sussex coleopterist, is to sieve leaf litter into a bag and stuff tissue paper into the top of the bag. The weevils are attracted to the dry tissue paper, where they can be easily spotted after a day or two. These ground-living weevils are part of the wood-decay community. The results of the 1995 survey suggest that although many wood-decay species appear to have disappeared from the wood, the remaining woodland retains several species of conservation interest, including the old nineteenth century favourite, *Trachodes hispidus*.

[*] In my experience the third species, *Acalles misellus*, occurs on aerial branches.

# Leicestershire and Rutland

It is not possible with total confidence to say that a particular species has become extinct. It would be easy to imagine announcing the loss of a species, only for some enthusiastic worker to rediscover it the next day. However, several of the species from Buddon Wood discussed above belong to one of two categories whose extinction in Leicestershire and Rutland is as sure as it ever can be. *Calosoma inquisitor* is an example of a large conspicuous beetle with well understood habits. It is unlikely to occur outside its favoured habitat and it is easy to find within that habitat, so the fact that nobody has found it for over fifty years suggests that it has disappeared. The ant nest beetles are examples of species that are dependent on a resource no longer present in Leicestershire. They cannot survive without that resource, so it is very unlikely that they are still there. The oil beetle, *Meloe proscarabaeus* is another large, conspicuous species that is likely to have disappeared from Leicestershire and Rutland. It is usually seen crawling over short turf in the spring and it was last seen at Barrowden in Rutland in 1943. It develops as a brood parasite in the nests of solitary bees. Many of the species that have been lost from the two counties share the characteristic of a specialist life history.

While it is prudent to be reticent in making too many claims for species extinctions, it is evident that a number of species have declined in numbers. It would, for example, require a great deal of effort nowadays to record the variety of dung species recorded by previous generations. Some species have proved to be sensitive to changes in the way that we manage the countryside. The Musk Beetle, *Aromia moschata*, and the weevil, *Cryptorhynchus lapathi*, are two striking beetles that were regarded in the nineteenth century as pests of osier beds. They were last recorded in Leicestershire in 1984 and 1945 respectively. This process of decline has probably been going on for at least two hundred years. The Vale of Belvoir is a landscape now dominated by intensive agriculture and one would expect to find few rare beetles even with a great deal of work. Yet Crabbe's eighteenth century list contains species, which were regarded as local or very local in 1907 and which would certainly now be regarded as rare.

But it is not all doom and gloom and species associated with several habitats have increased in numbers over the years. The construction of reservoirs toward the end of the nineteenth century created habitat that induced an explosion in numbers of two previously scarce ground beetles, *Blethisa multipunctata* and *Bembidion obliquum*, to the extent that Leicestershire became the source of most of the specimens of these two species in early twentieth century collections across the country. These two species still occur in Leicestershire though they have now abandoned the reservoirs and returned to their previous level of rarity. The reservoirs have since developed further habitats and Saddington Reservoir now supports a nationally important community of ground beetles and rove beetles associated with litter-rich fluctuating marsh. For this reason it was recently designated as a Site of Special Scientific Interest (SSSI) largely for its beetle fauna. Another previously unknown ground beetle, *Pterostichus quadrifoveolatus* was attracted to conifer plantations and heathland in the 1960s, when Harry Clements recorded it in numbers at five sites. Once again, this species failed to sustain its initial rate of increase and it was last recorded in Leicestershire in 1984. More recently, the proliferation of gravel pits across the county has resulted in an influx of immigrant water beetles that like pools of water on disturbed mineral substrates which warm up in the sunshine. Their colonisation of Leicestershire has been assisted by the general rise in temperatures that helps them fly to new habitats. In the future, we can expect to see more exotic species introduced through garden centres tand other entry points linked to global ravel. Several species from Australia, New Zealand, America and the Far East have been here for some time and are widely established and abundant in both the countryside and urban areas.

Leicestershire and Rutland provide habitat for several beetle communities of importance for nature conservation. Mature trees in hedgerows, gardens and mediaeval deer parks, such as Bradgate and Donington Parks support an astoundingly diverse wood-decay fauna that includes many national rarities. Litter-rich marsh that floods in the winter supports nationally important wetland beetle communities at Saddington Reservoir and in the Soar and Trent floodplains. Early successional sites with vegetation mosaics of bare ground and flower-rich grassland support a diverse beetle fauna in recently disused quarries, gravel pits and urban demolition sites. There is still plenty for future generations of coleopterists to occupy themselves with.

# *Notes on collections*

In recent times, the assembly of insect collections has attracted disapproval from some quarters, but it remains an essential element in the fields of beetle taxonomy, ecology and conservation. The collections of past coleopterists are especially valuable. Many old records are represented by names in publications and manuscripts that relate to species that have later been split or reinterpreted. In addition all coleopterists make occasional mistakes in identification and this tendency must have been more probable in times when identification keys were harder to use, when good quality microscopes and lighting were comparatively expensive and when access to good quality museum reference collections was difficult. Without a voucher specimen to check, these records have to be taken at face value, which often introduces a degree of doubt or uncertainty into the interpretation of faunal changes. The importance of collections as an irreplaceable resource for studying our past and present natural heritage is often underestimated. It would be short-sighted, if their curation and accessibility were to be compromised by the current crisis in financial resources for local government discretionary services.

It is unfortunate that many of the C19th Leicestershire collections have not survived intact apart from those of some eminent occasional visitors. The two main collections of Matthews and Frederick Bates were acquired by fellow private collectors who cherry-picked the rarities and dissipated or even threw away the remainder. Fortunately, all of the important C20th Leicestershire collections have been acquired by the local museum and are readily accessible, although some of them were damaged by insect pests before they were safely transferred. The Taylor collection was split when some of his weevils were sent to Peterborough Museum in exchange for the Crutwell collection and several named collections were split along with the entire museum service during local government reorganisation in 1997. In both cases Leicestershire specimens theoretically stayed in the county collection.

I list below what I know about the fate of Leicestershire collections.

## 19th Century collections

**Miss Arkwright**: A collection under this name is held by Leicestershire Museums Service (Acc. nos. 228-374'1898). It is without locality labels and is not associated with any supporting documentation.

**F. Bates**: On his death, Bates' collection was acquired by Donisthorpe who passed it on to G.W. Nicholson, then an enthusiastic beginner. Nicholson's interest in beetles never developed and it was then acquired by B.S. Williams, who assimilated some of the rarities into his own collection and gave the remainder to The Plant Pathology laboratory at Harpenden, now moved to York. The Williams collection is now at Liverpool Museum and there may well be Bates specimens there, although I did not notice any, when I spent two weeks there in 1985. I looked over the ground beetles at Harpenden in 1990 and there were a number of Bates' specimens there, though by no means anywhere near a complete set. Some specimens were labelled "F. Bates", but these included specimens collected after Bates' death, while other genuine Bates specimens were unlabelled. The localities will be difficult, probably impossible to identify from the labels that contain only numbers. Various bits of documentation have parted company with the collection at different times during its tortuous journey from owner to owner. Documents relating to early collecting passed with Donisthorpe's material to the Natural History Museum (London). Unfortunately, these appear to be of no use in interpreting the numbers on Bates' labels. The copy of Sharp's catalogue annotated with Leicestershire records passed from Williams to his son-in-law, Charles MacKechnie-Jarvis.

**H.W. Bates**: Much of the literature chronicling the destination of H.W. Bates' collection refers to his extensive foreign material. I have never come across any of his early Leicestershire specimens, but I have been told that there is some Bates material at Melbourne Museum, Australia, which arrived with MacLeay (H. Mendel, pers. comm.)

**F. Bouskell**: According to Donisthorpe, Bouskell's collection was destroyed in a fire (A.A. Allen, in litt.).

**C.T. Crutwell**: Crutwell's collection was acquired by exchange from Peterborough Museum by Leicestershire Museums (Acc. no. Z1197.1978)

**H. Donisthorpe**: Donisthorpe's collection, along with his collecting log is in the Natural History Museum (London).

**C.B. Headly**: Just over one quarter of Headly's original donation of 6,000 specimens of 1,300 species can still be identified in the museum collections (Brind 1980) (Acc. no. Z193.1909). It is possible that some of the remainder are represented by unlabelled material, but this is unlikely because of differences in mounting style. They are well labelled with locality data. Little documentation associated with his collection survives, but Headly's copy of Fowler passed to Taylor, then to Tozer and finally to Leicestershire Museums. It is annotated with Leicestershire records.

**H. Holyoak**: Destroyed; last seen in a pawnbroker's shop (Holyoak 1906).

**A. Matthews**: Matthews' collection was acquired by P.B. Mason, who cherry-picked the rarities for incorporation into his own collection. There is no trace of the remainder nor of any documentation. Mason's collection is now in Bolton Museum. I looked at part of Mason's collection in 1988 and was able to identify a small number of Matthews' specimens, despite the fact that they had been repinned presumably by Mason. All were positioned at the end of a series and had a high Mason catalogue number denoting late addition to the collection. The corresponding entries in Mason's catalogue did not always identify them as from Matthews' collection. Some of Matthews' specimens were on a characteristically shaped card. One was direct-pinned.

**F. Plant**: There is no record of what happened to Plant's collection after it was refused by Leicester Museum. I know of a single exchange specimen in the collections of the Natural History Museum (London).

**J.A. Power**: Power's collection, along with his collecting log is now in the Natural History Museum (London).

**J.H. Woolley**: A long series of specimens of many different species with no locality labels stands in the Taylor collection labelled in Taylor's handwriting with the number 1303. This number corresponds to an entry in Taylor's collection notebook dated 30th March 1942 explaining that they are from the J.H. Woolley collection. I assume that these are the remnants of the Woolley collection.

# 20th Century collections

**W.H. Barrow**: In the late 1950s, the beetle collections at Leicester Museum were rearranged into one integrated collection. The four main constituent collections at the time were given coloured labels in order to distinguish them. These coloured labels are now fading to the point where they are indistinguishable. One of the enduring mysteries to successive curators has been the origin of the collection given blue labels in the reorganisation (Acc. no. Z20.1954). This collection was acquired in 23 store boxes on 31st December 1953 from S.A. Taylor, after the death of his father, S.O. Taylor, in the previous September. S.A. Taylor died in a car crash just eight days later and his father's collection was acquired in an oak cabinet on 1st April 1954 from S.A. Taylor's widow. It was originally assumed that the collection in store boxes, later to be given blue labels, was that of S.A. Taylor. However, S.A. Taylor was primarily a botanist. According to Don Tozer, he never kept his own collection and it is highly likely that he collected beetles only on behalf of his father. I was told by W. Hunt that W.H. Barrow gave his collection to S.O. Taylor. The collection given blue labels is therefore more likely to be the remainder of Barrow's collection after some material had been incorporated into Taylor's own collection. A number of clues support this contention. The blue-labelled collection largely lacks locality labels, but the details of the few that do, carry Barrow's name. The pinning and mounting style is similar to Taylor's collection, as would be expected considering the close association of Taylor and Barrow right from the start of their collecting careers. Barrow was still alive in August 1945 when he sent Taylor some beetles from Barrowden *"out of a harvest wagon containing logs"*. At this time Barrow would have been nearly 90 years old and if he died soon after, his collection would have passed to Taylor not long before Taylor himself became ill and bed-ridden in 1949. On acquiring someone else's collection, it was normal practice to incorporate desiderata into your own collection and keep the remainder as spares. Some material was incorporated into Taylor's collection and the fact that the remainder remained intact is probably due, either to Taylor's subsequent early demise or because he always intended to donate them to the museum, which his son duly did.

**J.K. Bates**: Bates' collection is held by the Leicestershire Museums Service (Acc. no. Z25.1983).

**K.B. Clark**: Clark's collection has recently been acquired by the Leicestershire Museums Service.

**H.A.B. Clements**: I have a note that Clements' ground beetles (Carabidae) are with I.M. Evans, but the rest of his collection is held by the Leicestershire Museums Service. (Acc. no. Z333.1984)

**D.G. Goddard**: Goddard's collection remains with his widow.

**C.W. Henderson**: Henderson's collection is held by the Leicestershire Museums Service (Acc. no. Z90.1983). Henderson's collection is beautifully mounted and labelled in a uniform style. It is likely that he systematically relabelled his collection late in his collecting career. There is some evidence that he inadvertently got some labels mixed up, so they have to be interpreted with care.

**T.W. Tailby**: Tailby's collection is held by the Leicestershire Museums Service together with his collection notebooks (Acc. no. Z245.1968).

**S.O. Taylor**: Taylor's collection is held by the Leicestershire Museums Service together with his collection notebook (Acc. no. Z287.1954).

**D. Tozer**: Tozer's collection is held by the Leicestershire Museums Service together with his field and collection notebooks (Acc. no. Z97.1993 - see Forsythe 2004).

# *References*

ALEXANDER, K.N.A. & LOTT, D.A. (2001). A tribute to Don Goddard (1947-2000). *Coleopterist* **10**: 28-29.

ANON. (1876). *Leicester Town Museum. Fourth Report of the Museum Committee to the Town Council, to March 31 1876.* Leicester.

ANON. (1877). *Leicester Town Museum. Fifth Report of the Museum Committee to the Town Council, to March 31 1877.* Leicester.

ANON. (1880). *Leicester Town Museum. Eighth Report of the Museum Committee to the Town Council, to March 31 1880.* Leicester.

ANON. (1884). *Report of the Council of the Leicester Literary and Philosophical Society, presented to the Annual General Meeting, assembled June 23rd 1884.* Leicester.

ANON. (1885). *Report of the Council of the Leicester Literary and Philosophical Society, presented to the Annual General Meeting, assembled June 22nd 1885.* Leicester.

ANON. (1892). Major John Plant, F.G.S. *Geological Magazine* **29**: 286-288.

ANON. (1894). Report on societies. *Entomologist's Record* **5**: 88.

ANON. (1897). Report of section F for entomology 1897. *Transactions of the Leicester Literary and Philosophical Society* **5**: 21-24.

ANON. (1898). Current notes. *Entomologist's Record* **10**: 54.

ANON. (1905). Current notes. *Entomologist's Record* **17**: 109.

ANON. (1907). The British Association at Leicester. *Entomologist's Record* **19**: 258-259.

ANON. (1934). Report of section D, Botany, and section E, Zoology, Session 1933-34. *Transactions of the Leicester Literary and Philosophical Society* **33**: 41-43.

ANON. (1948). Report of botany, and biology sections. *Transactions of the Leicester Literary and Philosophical Society* **42**: 11.

ANON. (1952). Ald. Bouskell: solicitor-gardener. His death ends a Bosworth era. *Leicester Evening Mail* 2/2/1952: 6.

ASHURST, S. (1979). Untitled notes on S.O. and S.A. Taylor. MS held by Leicestershire Museums Service

BARROW, W.H. (1905). A Retrospect of a Season's Collecting Coleoptera, 1904. *Transactions of the Leicester Literary and Philosophical Society* **9**: 81-82.

BARROW, W.H. (1912). Capture of *Aleochara brunneipennis* near Leicester. *Entomologist's Record* **24**: 246.

BATES, F. (1849). Captures of coleopterous insects in light sandy situations. *Zoologist* **7**: 2437-2439.

BATES, F. (1852). Occurrence of *Necrodes littoralis* in considerable numbers. *Zoologist* **10**: 3376.

BATES, F. (1854). Captures in Leicestershire. *Zoologist* **12**: 4437-4438.

BATES, F. (1879). Midland entomology. *Midland Naturalist* **2**: 100.

BATES, F. (1892). Henry Walter Bates, F.R.S. *Proceedings of the Royal Geographical society, London* **14**: 245-247.

BATES, F. (1896). The Coleoptera of Bradgate Park. *Transactions of the Leicester Literary and Philosophical Society* **4**: 170-176.

BATES, H.W. (1843). Notes on coleopterous insects frequenting damp places. *Zoologist* **1**: 114-115.

BATES, H.W. (1844a). Notes on the habits of Coleoptera. *Zoologist* **2**: 410-412.

BATES, H.W. (1844b). Note on the captures of rarer Coleoptera in Leicestershire. *Zoologist* **2**: 699-700.

BLAIR, K.G. (1951). Obituary – Horace St. John Kelly Donisthorpe. *Entomologist's monthly Magazine* **87**: 215.

BOUSKELL, F. (1893). Leicester Entomological Club. *Entomologist's Record* **4**: 163-164.

BOUSKELL, F. (1898). Leicestershire Coleoptera in 1897. *Entomologist's Record* **10**: 19-22.

BOUSKELL, F. (1901). The Variation and Distribution of the genus *Aphodius* (Illiger). *Transactions of the Leicester Literary and Philosophical Society* **5**: 571-605.

BOUSKELL, F. (1903a). *Tetropium castaneum*, L. – a species of longicorn Coleoptera new to Britain. *Entomologist's Record* **15**: 288.

BOUSKELL, F. (1903b). Reports of the Sections: Section "F" Entomology. *Transactions of the Leicester Literary and Philosophical Society* **7**: 149-151.

BOUSKELL, F. (1907). Insects. In PAGE, W. (ed.), *The Victoria History of the County of Rutland* **1**. London: Archibald Constable pp 64-94.

BOUSKELL, F. in ANON. (1951). Obituary – Horace St. John Kelly Donisthorpe, F.Z.S., F.R.E.S. *Entomologist's Record* **63**: 228.

BRIND, R. (1980). Report on C.B. Headly and his association with Leicester Museum. MS report to Leicestershire Museums Service

CLEMENTS, H.A.B. & EVANS, I.M. (1973). Leicestershire bugs. *Transactions of the Leicester Literary and Philosophical Society* **47**: 50-68.

COLLINGWOOD, C.A. (1957). Myrmecophilous beetles in the Midlands. *Entomologist's Record* **69**: 10-14.

CRABBE, G. (1790). The Natural History of the Vale of Belvoir. In: J. Nichols, *Additional collections towards The History and Antiquities of the Town and County of Leicester*, pp. 1256-1291.

CRABBE, G. (1795). The Natural History of the Vale of Belvoir. In: *Nichols' History of the Antiquities of the County of Leicester* **1**: 191-208.

CROCKER, J. (ed.) (1981). *Charnwood Forest: a Changing Landscape*. Loughborough: Loughborough Naturalists' Club.

CROCKER, J. & DAWS, J. (1996). *Spiders of Leicestershire and Rutland*. Newtown Linford: Kairos Press.

CROCKER, J. & DAWS, J. (2001). *Spiders of Leicestershire and Rutland Millennium Atlas*. Newtown Linford: Kairos Press.

DARBY, M. (2006). *Biographical Dictionary of British Coleopterists* published on www.coleopterist.org.uk.

DIXEY, F.A. (1911). Obituary. *Entomologist's Record* **23**: 183-184.

DIXON, G.B. (1905). Quarterly Reports of the Sections: Section F for Entomology. *Transactions of the Leicester Literary and Philosophical Society* **9**: 81-90.

DONISTHORPE, H.StJ.K. (1896). Untitled. In: Quarterly reports of the sections – section E Entomology. *Transactions of the Leicester Literary and Philosophical Society* **4**: 198-200.

DONISTHORPE, H.StJ.K. (1903). Frederick Bates, F.E.S. etc. *Entomologist's Record*. **15**: 347-349.

DONISTHORPE, H.StJ.K. (1927). *The Guests of British Ants*. London: Routledge.

DONISTHORPE, H.StJ.K. (1941). Coleoptera in Leicestershire. *Entomologist's Record*. **53**: 132-133.

DOUGLAS, R.N. (1908). Insects. In PAGE, W. (ed.), *The Victoria History of the County of Rutland* **1**. London: Archibald Constable pp 39-45.

DUFFY, E.A.J. (1947). A contribution towards the Biology of *Aromia moschata L. the "Musk" Beetle. Proceedings of the South London entomological and Natural History Society.* **1947-1948**: 82-110.

DUNNING, J.W. (1886). John Arthur Power. *Entomologist.* **19**: 193-200.

EVANS, I.M. (1983). Notes on conversation with D. Tozer 6.12.83. MS held by Leicestershire Museums Service.

FORSYTHE, T.G. (2004). The Donald Tozer collection. *Coleopterist* **13**: 148.

FOWLER, W.W. (1892). Obituary – John Thomas Harris F.E.S. *Entomologist's monthly Magazine* **28**: 291.

FOWLER, W.W. (1897). Obituary – The Rev. Andrew Matthews. *Entomologist's monthly Magazine* **33**: 258-260.

FOWLER, W.W. (1900). Obituary – William Gabriel Blatch F.E.S. *Entomologist's monthly Magazine* **36**: 89-90.

FOWLER, W.W. (1911). Obituary – Canon C.T. Crutwell. *Entomologist's monthly Magazine* **47**: 114.

FOWLER, W.W. & DONISTHORPE, H.StJ.K. (1913). *The Coleoptera of the British Islands.* (volume 6) London: L. Reeve & Co.

HARLEY, J. (1840). Catalogue of the land birds of Leicestershire. In: W. MACGILLIVRAY. *A History of British Birds Indigenous and Migratory.* London: Scott, Webster & Geary.

HENDERSON, C.W. (1962). An introduction to the beetles of Bradgate Park and Reservoir. In ANON. *Bradgate Park and Cropston Reservoir margins* Loughborough: Loughborough Naturalists' Club.

HENDERSON, C.W. (1975). The beetles of Buddon Wood. MS held by Leicestershire Museums Service.

HOLYOAK, H. (1906). Fifty years' entomological reminiscences. *Transactions of the Leicester Literary and Philosophical Society* **10**: 55-59.

HONEYBONE, M. (1987). *The Vale of Belvoir.* Buckingham: Barracuda Books.

HORWOOD, A.R. & NOEL, C.W.F. (1933). *The Flora of Leicestershire and Rutland.* Oxford: Oxford University Press

HUDLESTON, W.H. (1894). The anniversary address of the President. "John Plant". *Proceedings of the Geological Society of London* **1893-1894**: 52-53.

JANSON, E.W. (1857). New British species noted in 1856. Postscript. *Entomologist's Annual* **1857**: 84.

JEEVES, M. (ed.) (1996). Buddon Wood: an ecological survey. Unpublished report by Leicestershire Wildlife Consultancy for Redland Aggregates Ltd.

KIRBY, H.B. (1845). Capture of coleopterous insects in Leicestershire. *Zoologist* **3**: 1094.

LISNEY, A.A. (1960). *A Bibliography of British Lepidoptera 1608 – 1799.* London : Chiswick Press.

LLOYD, R.W. (1951). Obituary – Horace St. John Kelly Donisthorpe. *Entomologist's monthly Magazine* **87**: 215.

LOTT, F.B. (1935). *The Centenary Book of the Leicester Literary and Philosophical Society.* Leicester: Leicester Literary and Philosophical Society.

LOTT, D.A. (1984). Report on visit to Mr. W. Hunt, 9th May 1984. MS held by Leicestershire Museums Service.

LOTT, D.A. (1994). Obituary – Donald Tozer. *Coleopterist* **2**: 88.

LOWE, E.E., MAYES, W.E., WAGSTAFFE, R. & TAYLOR, S.O. (1933). The zoology of Leicestershire. In: BRYAN, P.W. (ed.) *A Scientific Study of Leicester and District.* London: British Association for the Advancement of Science.

MACKECHNIE JARVIS, C. (1976). A history of the British Coleoptera. *Proceedings of the British Entomological and Natural History Society.* **8**: 91-112.

MARREN, P. (2008). Darwin's war-horse: beetle-collecting in 19th-century England. *British Wildlife* **19**: 153-159.

MARSHALL (1790). The Rural Economy of the Midland counties (2 vols.). London: John Nichols.

MARSHAM, T. (1802). *Coleoptera Britannica, sistens Insecta Coleoptera Britaniæ indigena, &c.* London: Londini.

MONTAGU BROWN, A. (1889). *The Vertebrate Animals of Leicestershire and Rutland.* Birmingham.

MOON, H.P. (1976). *Henry Walter Bates F.R.S. Explorer, Scientist and Darwinian.* Leicester: Leicestershire Museums, Art Galleries and Records Service.

MOTT, F.T. (1878). Artisan naturalists. *Midland Naturalist* **1**: 310-311.

MOTT, F.T. (1887). On Mr John Plant's catalogue of Leicestershire Mollusca. *Transactions of the Leicester Literary and Philosophical Society* **2**: 198-200.

PLANT, F. (1857). Captures of Coleoptera in Leicestershire. *Zoologist* **15**: 5544-5545.

PLANT, F. (1863). Letter to Samuel Stevens. *Zoologist* **21**: 8398.

PLANT, J. (1844a) *Zoologist* **2**: 473.

PLANT, J. (1844b). Note on the comparative numbers of Coleoptera affecting meadow lands. *Zoologist* **2**: 475-476.

PRIMAVESI, A.L. & EVANS, P.A. (eds.) (1988). *Flora of Leicestershire.* Leicester: Leicestershire Museums, Art Galleries and Records Service

QUILTER, H.E. (1887). The metamorphoses of *Galeruca nymphea* Lin. *Transactions of the Leicester Literary and Philosophical Society* **1**: 17-20.

ROBSON, G. (1879). The predaceous water beetles (Hydradephaga) of Leicestershire. *Midland Naturalist* **2**: 57-60.

ROEBUCK, A. (1938). Beetles in a church.*Entomologist's monthly Magazine* **74**: 209.

ROEBUCK, A. & BROADBENT, L. (1945). Some notes on *Cryptohypnus quadripustulatus* F. on grass fields in the Midlands. *Entomologist's monthly Magazine* **81**: 8.

RYE,B.G. & SKINNER, P.F. (1895). Coleoptera in 1894. *Entomologist's monthly Magazine* **30**: 276-277.

SALMON, M.A. & WAKEHAM-DAWSON, A. (1999). Thomas Vernon Wollaston and the Madeiran butterfly fauna – a re-appraisal. *British Journal of Entomology and Natural History* **12**: 69-88.

SCUDDER, G.G.E. (1956). Additions to the county distribution tables of the British Hemiptera - Heteroptera. *Entomologist's monthly Magazine* **93**: 49-51.

SHIRT, D.B. (ed.) 1987. *British Red Data Books: 2. Insects.* Peterborough: Nature Conservancy Council.

SMITH, K.G.V & BATES, J.K. (1956). Some records of Ocypta interrupta Mg. (Dipt., Tachinidae). *Entomologist's monthly Magazine* **92**: 22.

SQUIRES, A.E. & JEEVES, M. (1994). *Leicestershire and Rutland Woodlands past and present.* Leicester: Kairos Press.

STEPHENS, J.F. (1828). *Illustrations of British Entomology. Mandibulata.* **1**. London.

STEPHENS, J.F. (1839). *A Manual of British Coleoptera, or Beetles.* London.

STEVENSON, J. & SQUIRES, A.E. (1994). *Bradgate Park Childhood Home of Lady Jane Grey.* Leicester: Kairos Press.

TAYLOR, S.O. (1942). Question of gravity. *Entomologist's monthly Magazine* **78**: 118.

THOMAS, K. (1983). *Man and the Natural World. Changing Attitudes in England 1500-1800.* London: Allen Lane.

TINDALL, A.R. (1943). Records of Coleoptera at South Wigston, Leicester. *Entomologist's monthly Magazine* **79**: 113.

TINDALL, A.R. (1959). A note on *Cricotopus trifasciatus* Mg. (Dipt., Chironomidae) and the pupae of *Triaenodes bicolor* Curtis (Trich., Leptoceridae). *Entomologist's monthly Magazine* **79**: 113.

VICE, W.A. (1896). Report of section F for entomology 1896. *Transactions of the Leicester Literary and Philosophical Society* **4**: 21-23.

WALKER, J.J. (1923). In memoriam – The Rev. Canon W.W. Fowler, D.Sc., M.A., F.L.S. *Entomologist's monthly Magazine* **59**: 150.

WALLACE, A.R. (1905). *My Life.* London: Chapman & Hall.

WESTWOOD, J.O. (1844). Notice of the occurrence of the coleopterous genus *Serropalpus* in Leicestershire. *Zoologist* **2**: 701.

WHITTINGHAM, W.G. (1908). Reports of the Sections: Section "F" Entomology. *Transactions of the Leicester Literary and Philosophical Society* **12**: 243-244.

WOOLLEY, J.H. (1895a). Beetle collecting in November. N*aturalist's Journal* **4**: 43.

WOOLLEY, J.H. (1895b). Strawberries, beetles and hedgehogs. *Naturalist's Journal* **4**: 251-252.

# *Index*

*Melandrya caraboides*, 46
*Melasis buprestoides*, 46
Mendel, Howard, 37, 39
*Micrelus ericae*, 41
Minotaur Beetle, 41
Misterton, 7
*Monotoma angusticollis*, 45
*Monotoma conicicollis*, 45
Moon, Prof. H.P., 29
Moore, J.D., 10
Moss, W., 22, 25
Moths, 12, 15, 19, 27, 36, 38
Mott, F.T., 13
Musk Beetle, 2, 12, 47
*Mycetophagus piceus*, 43
*Myrmetes piceus*, 45
Natural History Museum (London), 8, 37, 49, 50
*Necrodes littoralis*, 7
*Neliocarus faber*, 41
*Neliocarus nebulosus*, 41
*Nemadus colonoides*, 43
New Forest, 12, 19, 21, 23
*Nossidium pilosellum*, 43
*Notiophilus aquaticus*, 41
*Notolaemus unifasciatus*, 43
*Notothecta flavipes*, 45
*Ochthebius exsculptus*, 42
*Ochthephilum fracticorne*, 42
Oil beetles, 2, 47
Oram, 14, 17
*Orchesia micans*, 46
*Orchesia minor*, 16
*Orthocerus clavicornis*, 41
Osborne, R.D., 37
*Otiorhynchus ovatus*, 41
Outwoods, 14
Owston Wood, 19
Oxford University Museum, 12
*Oxypoda formiceticola*, 45
*Oxypoda recondita*, 43, 45
*Phloeopora concolor*, 20
*Phloiotrya vaudoueri*, 43
*Phymatodes testaceus*, 43
Pigg, Thomas, 8
Pill beetles, 41
Plant, Francis, 7, 9, 10, 12, 44, 50

Plant, John, 5, 6, 7, 8, 10
Plant, Nathaniel, 9
*Plectophloeus nitidus*, 43
*Podabrus alpinus*, 45
*Poecilium alni*, 46
Power, J. A., 8, 10, 40, 50
*Prionocyphon serricornis*, 46
*Ptenidium brenskei*, 42
*Ptenidium formicetorum*, 45
*Ptenidium gressneri*, 46
*Pterostichus quadrifoveolatus*, 47
*Ptinella errabunda*, 44
*Quedius brevis*, 45
Quilter, H.E., 14, 15, 17
Reed beetles, 7, 43
*Rhagonycha translucida*, 45
Rhinoceros Beetle, 43
*Rhinoncus castor*, 41
River Lin, 40, 42
River Soar, 36, 38, 48
Robson, George, 13, 14, 17
Roebuck, A., 29, 33
Rove beetle, 13, 15, 16, 21, 27, 30, 42, 45, 47
Rowley, F., 19
Rutland Natural History Society, 36
Rye, B.G., 19, 25
Saddington Reservoir, 16, 47, 48
*Scaphisoma boleti*, 43
Scottish National Museum, 23
*Selatosomus aeneus*, 41
Serica brunnea, 41
Sessile Oak, 44
Sheet Hedges Wood, 5, 14
Shenton Hall, 8
Sherwood Forest, 15, 24
Small-leaved Lime, 44
South Wigston, 29
Sowter, F.A., 31
*Sphaerius acaroides*, 15
*Sphindus dubius*, 30
Spiders, 14, 36
Squires, Tony, 36, 44
Stag Beetle, 2
Stag Beetle, Lesser, 2
Stanyon, 15
*Stenichnus godarti*, 45

## OBITUARY

**DONALD TOZER** - Don Tozer, known to many coleopterists in the Amateur Entomologist's Society, died in October, 1993, after a short illness following a stroke.

He was born on 12th April, 1907 and went to Wyggestons School in Leicester where he met his life-long friend and collecting companion, Claude Henderson. On leaving school he joined his father as a painter and decorator, an occupation that he followed all his working life.

His interest in insects began at an early age. While he and Claude Henderson were visiting Leicester Museum they met S. O. Taylor, a local coleopterist, who inspired them to take up the pursuit of beetles. A list of rare beetles captured by Mr Donald Tozer in 1925 appeared in the Transactions of the Leicester Literary and Philosophical Society. He was one of the founder members of the Amateur Entomologist's Society as attested by his membership number, 36, and he served on the beetle identification panel right up until his death. Many beginners in the study of beetles have benefitted from his help and generosity with specimens.

Don was severely lame after contracting polio in childhood and he relied very much on his bicycle and motor-bike to get around. His favoured collecting areas were mainly local and included Leicestershire, Sherwood Forest and the Peterborough area. He had an uncanny knack of picking up rare species, often on roadside verges and hedges. In 1939 he discovered *Agrilus pannonicus* (Piller & Mitterpacher) in Sherwood Forest. Between 1943 and 1947 he wrote several short notes, published in the Entomologist's Monthly Magazine. Later he made important contributions to the Monks Wood list. Apart from his Coleoptera collections he also built up an outstanding Lepidoptera collection, composed mainly of bred specimens, and several of his records appear in the Leicestershire Heteroptera list.

Don was also a prolific breeder of beetles. He once brought back several *Chrysolina menthastri* (Suffrian) from a trip to Hampshire. These he released into his garden where they became well established on his garden mint and thrived for many years. For several years after, his advice as the local beetle expert was sought by anxious neighbours in dealing with a strange new pest that was eating their mint. Don never let on how they got there.

Don was a good-natured character and visitors were always greeted with a mug of tea and pleasant conversation. In later years, he became increasingly disheartened by changes in the countryside which he held responsible for an evident decrease in insect populations. Despite that, he continued collecting and maintained an interest in beetles up until the last years of his life. He always retained a character of independence and it was fortunate that he was able to remain living in his own house until his final illness.

Don's Coleoptera collection, field notebooks and correspondence have kindly been donated to Leicestershire Museums Service by Mr John Dacey, his nephew. His Lepidoptera collections were sold at auction by Churchgate Antiques, Leicester, on November 12th 1993.

D. A. Lott

Leicestershire Museums Service, 96 New Walk, Leicester LE1 6TD.